Morehead

THE COOKBOOK DECODER

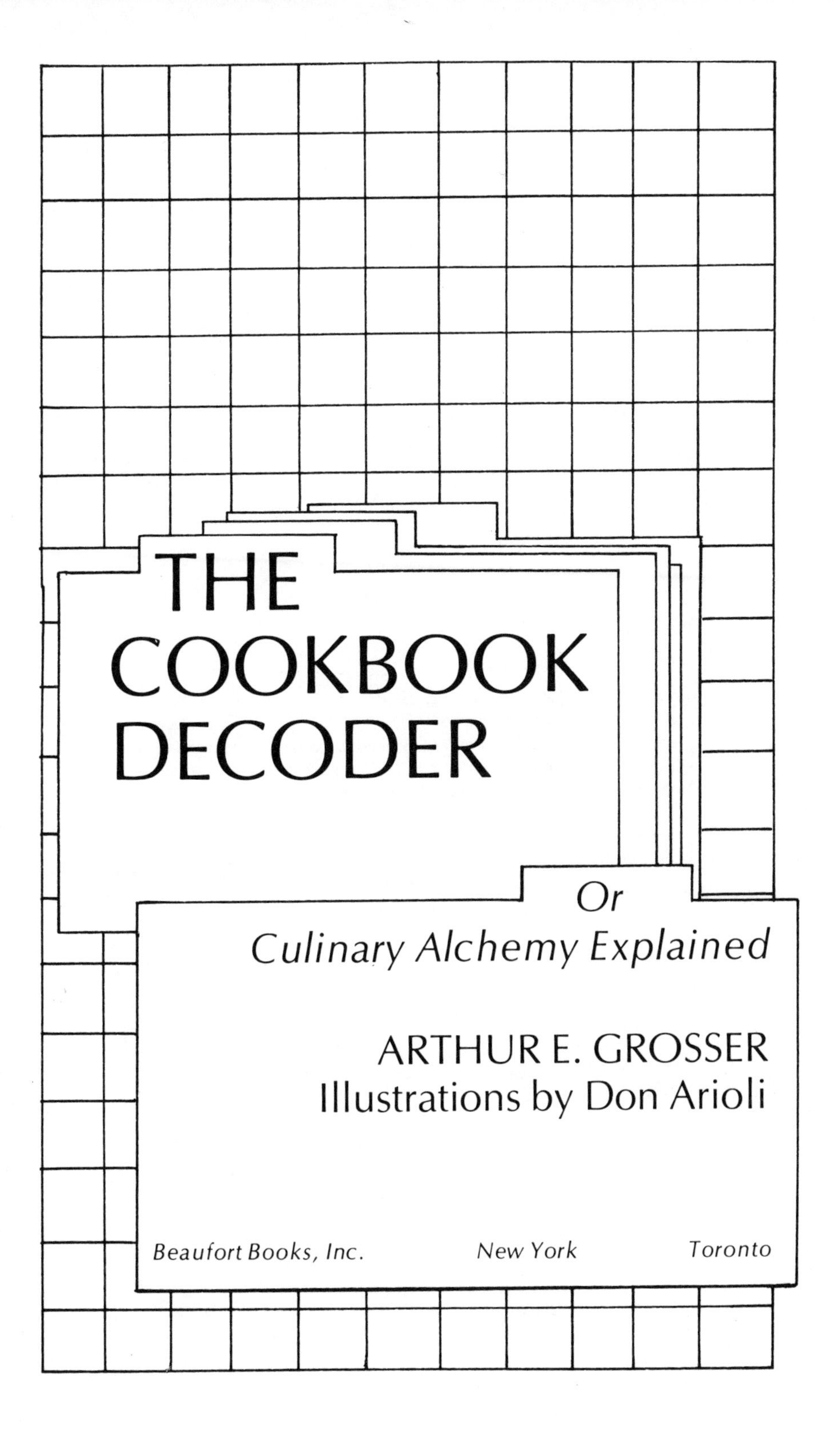

THE COOKBOOK DECODER

Or

Culinary Alchemy Explained

ARTHUR E. GROSSER

Illustrations by Don Arioli

Beaufort Books, Inc. *New York* *Toronto*

Library of Congress Cataloging in Publication Data

Grosser, Arthur E., 1934 –
The cookbook decoder.

Includes index.
1. Cookery. I. Title.
TX652.G75 1981 641.5 81-2143
ISBN 0-8253-0033-9 AACR2

Published in the United States by Beaufort Books, Inc., New York.
Published simultaneously in Canada by General Publishing Co. Limited

Designed by Joy Chu
Printed in the U.S.A. First Edition

10 9 8 7 6 5 4 3 2 1

CONTENTS

ACKNOWLEDGMENTS

My fond thanks to my professional colleagues for their expertise and scientific flights of inspired fancy when faced with a chemical impasse. In particular I am indebted to Professors M. Hegsted and R. H. Common.

I am also grateful to a band of students who cooked up many of my recipes and gave me the undiluted feedback. Especially helpful were Jean Brady, Pierre Madden, Bronwen Mantel, Donna Oswald, and Siriwan Ratanathanawongs. They were supplemented by friends and acquaintances who, though not passionate or professional about food, couldn't cook or eat without using their heads. They suggested culinary curiosities or strange quirks in recipes and dispatched me to my kitchen with tasks of verification and understanding.

If you, dear reader, are like them, send along your perplexities or explanations. Meanwhile, *bon appetit*.

A.E.G.

Avoide your Bokes written of Receipts,
For all such Receipts are full of Deceipts;
Trust not such Receipts, and lerne well this Clause,
Nothing is wrought but by his proper Cause:
Wherefore that practice falleth farr behinde
Wher knowledge of the cause is not in minde:
Therefor remember ever more wisely,
That you woorke nothing but you knowe and whie.

Thomas Norton, *Ordinall of Alchimy (1652)*

INTRODUCTION

I never understood my first cooking lesson. I was six and had chicken pox, and my mother, having exhausted all other entertainments, began to explain how to boil an egg. The water must be salted. "It's to keep them from cracking." She regarded the egg. "But they still crack." We pondered this for a moment, then I nodded. Whether it cracked or not, obviously an egg had to be pacified by an offering of salt.

Many years later, cooking dinner on my illegal hot plate in the dorm, fresh from lectures which purported to train us for rational, cold-blooded, objective analysis, I would do a strange thing: toss in salt along with the egg. I was as superstitious as Stone Age man. After all, why take a chance? Just follow every recipe instruction to the letter, and all will be well with the world.

A fantastic gourmet dish, guaranteed to elevate my social status with my delightful dinner guest, would reluctantly be rejected if it called for a wooden spoon, and I had only metal. A metal dish is called for in the next recipe, but the pantry has only glass? Back to the recipe hunt. Ultimately something had to be done to bring these tyrannical recipes to heel.

The only way seemed to be to discover the underlying logic of the recipes, the "why" behind the directions. As a student of chemistry, I discovered that "following the recipe" was boring and frustrating. I had to learn the principles that lay behind the instructions. Otherwise I wasted a lot of time by overlooking an obvious shortcut, or I bungled the whole job with an improper substitution. *The Cookbook Decoder* is the result of that search for a rationale of cooking.

Cooking is the oldest, most basic, and most universal human

application of physical and chemical changes to natural materials. Over the years, culinary recipes have come to conform to a simple logic. That logic is science, and we practice it every day we cook.

By analyzing more than twenty do-it-yourself kitchen demonstrations and more than a hundred recipes, *The Cookbook Decoder* will explain how what we do in the kitchen affects the texture, color, and flavor of our food.

But a mere collection of unrelated facts will leave us just as dependent as before. The *Decoder*'s aim is to provide the reader with a framework for *thinking about* and modifying recipes with some degree of self-assurance. And this is easy to do, for every cook is a practicing food chemist with enormous unconscious chemical expertise. *The Cookbook Decoder* helps you recover this experience, rationalize it, and put it in your service.

You will learn why these recipes, from the most elementary — we start with the boiled egg — to highly challenging concoctions, demand specific sequences, temperatures, times, unusual ways of mixing ingredients, and special utensils. The essential (or interesting) ingredient or direction in each recipe is noted (by italics or a □) and explained. There is also a résumé at the end of each chapter, so you can get at these ideas easily.

To what end all this knowledge? So that you will be able to ad-lib with recipes, retaining the necessary and omitting the frivolous, and thus to make your own recipes — to satisfy your curiosity, astound your friends and enemies with your culinary erudition, and put you in command, if not of your entire life, then at least of your cooking.

Unless otherwise noted, all recipes yield six portions.

The metric equivalents are given in the Appendix, and are included in the recipes for packaged goods only.

1

THE EGG: A NOBLE BEAST

BOILED EGGS

In our folklore, the newlywed who can't cook an egg is exceeded in domestic incompetence only by the toast burner. It would be simple enough to boil an egg if eggs didn't have the unpleasant habit of cracking and leaving messy white streamers in the pot. The modest egg has elaborate self-defense mechanisms — an infuriating resistance to peeling at a picnic or an appetite-quenching gray-green layer on the hard-cooked yolk. All this when merely *boiling* an egg.

But it is not surprising. Eggs have deceptively simple exteriors, but they are complicated biochemical systems and lack only the trigger of fertilization to start the orderly assembly of molecular building blocks that results in a chick. If you muck about with a complex chemical system, unexpected things can happen.

Let's start with the first simple catastrophe — cracking. Why do eggs crack and can we do anything about it? Are some recipes better than others in preventing it?

Eggs crack when boiled because they are built to do so. They carry around a little heat-sensitive detonator. Here's the proof.

AUTODEMONSTRATION A

Heat an egg in a pot of cold water and watch the large end. You will see a stream of air bubbles coming through the shell from a pocket of air held captive between membranes in the egg.

As the egg heats up, the air inside expands and tries to find a way out of the shell. Cleverly foreseeing this eventuality, the egg has provided itself with an escape hatch: pores in the large end of the shell. The air bubbles you saw in the Autodemonstration had forced their way through these tiny holes in the eggshell.

Now a race begins between pressure buildup within the egg and its release as the air oozes out. If the air pocket is heated faster than the air can escape through the shell, there is terrific internal pressure, and the shell cracks.

Egg structure

But not every egg, like not every person, will crack under stress. Some eggshells have bigger pores than others, let the air out more readily, and are relatively uncrackable. And some don't have a large air pocket. But there is no way of knowing which is which beforehand, so recipes have developed lots of anticracking devices, one of which is to poke a hole in the large end of the shell. The next demonstration will show you why this is a good idea.

AUTODEMONSTRATION B

Put a hole in the large end of an egg. (Use the egg from Autodemostration A.) Don't be nervous; the hole can be pretty big, even ⅛ inch. Then proceed as in the first demonstration. Start in cold water and heat up. You will see not little bubbles but a jet of air expelled from the hole.

Now let's apply these ideas in a simple recipe.

1. SOFT-COOKED AND HARD-COOKED EGGS
(one serving)

2 eggs at room temperature
1 quart *cold* water
□ 2 tablespoons salt

Make a hole in the *large end* of each egg. (A thumbtack can substitute for the more expensive items sold in gourmet shops for this purpose.) The hole should be 1/16 to ⅛ inch in diameter.

Put the eggs into a pot with the water and *salt*. Add more water (and salt) if necessary to cover the eggs. Heat the pot until the water boils, then reduce the heat so that the water *simmers*.

There's a bit more to this recipe (on page 7), but let's stop here and examine it so far.

The whole idea behind crack prevention is making sure the air is valved through the shell before the pressure builds up. This recipe starts the eggs in cold water, so their temperature will rise gradually and the air will have more time to seep out. Reducing the heat to simmering helps as well and prevents overcooking, which toughens the white before the yolk has cooked.

There is an aesthetic bonus hidden in the boiled-egg recipe. Egg white will cook very quickly, and if it sets into shape before the air gets out, the shelled egg has a flat end like a boxer's nose. The pinholed egg, on the other hand, mirrors the beautiful oval shape of the shell, because the white flowed into the space vacated by the escaping air. Of course a flat bottom may be useful if eggs sitting "at attention" is what you are after.

Pinholing is a good precaution when dealing with old eggs. As an egg ages, more air gets into it, and the air pocket enlarges, sometimes enough to float the eggs in water. These floaters are best used for scrambled eggs.

But sometimes it's terribly inconvenient to start eggs in cold water. If the pot's too small to cook them all in one batch, it seems silly to throw out the hot water and start all over again. But an egg started in hot water can bring another cracking mechanism into play — thermal shock.

In human terms, thermal shock is what happens when the hot water suddenly gives out in the middle of your shower. It is also what happens to a piece of common glass when it is put into a hot oven directly from the freezer. Almost all materials expand as their temperature rises, and when this happens too fast, a brittle substance shatters.

When a refrigerator-cold egg is tossed into boiling water, the different regions of the shell, which are of different thicknesses, cannot expand in unison, and the shell cracks. So, if you must put the eggs in hot water, use the pinhole trick, and then run some warm tapwater over them to lessen the shock when they are put in the pot.

And then put in some salt!

Unreasonable? Illogical?

At first glance it does seem ridiculous. Although air can get in and out of the eggshell, salt cannot, so what effect can it have on the egg snug inside?

It does raise the temperature of the boiling water a bit, but not enough to be important. And it does not prevent cracking, which can happen to even the best laid and most apprehensively watched eggs. So why add salt?

If eggs crack while cooking in *salted* water, there are, magically, no ugly streamers of white floating about. The white coagulates at the crack and seals the opening. Hence, salting the water is a sort of first aid for a ruptured egg.

Egg white is almost all water (88 percent) and protein (11 percent). In its natural state the white is semifluid, and when cooked it becomes firm but resilient. This change mirrors on a visible level the fate of molecules when we turn up the heat.

An egg protein is a shy molecule, and when left alone will curl up into itself, coiling into a ball. Held in this shape by very weak chemical bonds inside the ball, it is content to examine its navel and floats leisurely around the 88-percent sea, without any interest in any other protein balls. This leisured, snobbish existence is destroyed if the temperature is raised.

Then, hordes of water molecules carom off each other and the proteins in frenzied and chaotic collisions. As the temperature goes higher, the action becomes more energetic until a molecular demolition derby is under way. The weak internal bonds of the egg protein cannot hold the ball together, and it opens out into a floppy streamer.

Only now do we find the real reason for the protein's solitary behavior. It coiled itself up not from narcissism, but as a defensive maneuver; for when it has opened out into a streamer, it exposes a "soft underbelly" of richly seductive targets for chemical attack and bonding. As these protein streamers bump into each other, they immediately bond and form strong links; others latch on randomly as well, until finally there is a three-dimensional protein network, semirigid and immobile—to our touch, firm and resilient. The difference between the semifluid raw egg and the semirigid cooked one is just the difference between the natural "sea state" of the protein balls and the network that heating has driven them into.

Egg proteins attach

Finally a random network is formed by these floppy molecules.

Egg protein network

Not only will high temperature and the consequent molecular massage pummel the solitary protein molecules, opening them up and allowing them to form a network, so will salt or food acids. Chemical bonds are electrical, and the charged particles from *dissolved salt or acid* (lemon juice, vinegar) can change the electrical environment about the solitary proteins so much that their weak internal bonds break spontaneously. They then uncoil and enter the dance that leads to the interlocking molecular network. In other words, the protein cooks a lot faster.

This is the reason the dissolved salt or acid in the cooking water helps keep a cracked egg neat — it makes the cooking water much more efficient and faster at its job. If the egg cracks, the white is cooked at the crack and seals it right away, an instantaneous self-repair job.

In a few paragraphs we'll see how recipes use this trick when poaching eggs.

But there is another pitfall to avoid when hard-cooking eggs — the dreaded green yolk. How does a beautiful white and yellow egg get such a bilious coating on its innermost parts?

The egg does it to itself, really, but we help it along with overcooking. As the egg is warmed, a small portion of the protein in the white decomposes, and its sulfur and hydrogen unite to form hydrogen sulfide gas, which has a deservedly bad name as "the smell of rotten eggs." The egg is not rotting, just cooking.

This gas generated in the white collects in the coolest part of the egg, which right now is in the center, where the yolk is. Yolks contain iron, which has a terrific attraction for sulfur. The fickle iron kicks out the hydrogen and forms solid iron sulfide. This union is so swift and tempestuous that it happens at the first opportunity — when the gas reaches the surface of the yolk and forms the dark iron-sulfide deposit.

You can prevent this unnatural liaison by using cold water. Here's the rest of our first recipe:

1. SOFT-COOKED AND HARD-COOKED EGGS (continued)

Cook 2 to 3 minutes for soft-cooked, and 10 to 12 minutes for hard-cooked. Immediately remove the pot from the heat, put it in the sink, and *let cold water run into it until the eggs are cool* enough to handle. Shell them and serve.

The cold-water bath not only prevents overcooking (which gives the reaction more time for dirty work), it quenches it altogether. After ten minutes' cooking, the egg is heated through, and by chilling the shell in cold water, we force the hydrogen sulfide gas to collect there, pulling it away from the iron-laden yolk.

(a) As cooking starts
(b) Toward end of cooking
(c) Immersed in cold water

Green deposit on yolk

Aging does a lot of terrible things to eggs: their air pockets enlarge so much they may end up as "floaters"; they develop green yolk deposit a lot faster than fresh ones; their whites get slack and watery, rendering them unfit for service as poached or fried eggs. And their grade goes down.

Eggs are evaluated by weight (or size) *and* quality (grade). No matter how good an egg the hen lays, its quality will decay as it stands around. So use your freshest eggs for poaching and frying and reserve the others for noncrucial jobs like scrambling or baking.

Another technique for boiling eggs is to use an egg coddler, which is just a cup (usually ceramic) with a screw-on lid. You can make one yourself from a glass jar, but if you do, remember to put a pinhole in the lid. Expanding air can break an eggshell, and it can also explode weak glass jars.

2. CODDLED EGGS
(one serving)

2 eggs
¼ teaspoon butter
⅛ teaspoon salt
⅛ teaspoon pepper
3 small mushrooms, chopped
1 tablespoon Parmesan cheese

Grease the inside of the coddler with butter. Break one egg into it carefully, making sure the yolk does not break. Add half the salt and pepper, break in the second egg, then the remaining salt and pepper. Set a layer of mushrooms on top, cover with the cheese and screw on the lid.

Immerse the coddler in boiling water for 12 to 15 minutes. Remove the coddler from the pot, unscrew the lid, and serve in the coddler.

For variety, one can add flaked fish, grated cheese, chopped ham, herbs, sliced mushrooms, etc., to the coddler along with the salt and pepper.

Here is a nice way to use our skill at hard-cooking. Stuffed eggs are elegant but very simple, and when served with vegetables like cold cooked asparagus and tomato, make a light, refreshing dish.

3. STUFFED EGGS

12 hard-cooked eggs, halved
3 tablespoons mayonnaise
½ teaspoon salt
¼ teaspoon pepper
1 tablespoon hot mustard
1⅓ tablespoons prepared horseradish
6 strips well-cooked bacon, crumbled
12 ½-inch squares of pimento

Remove the egg yolks from the egg halves and put them in a bowl with the mayonnaise, salt, pepper, horseradish, and mustard. Mash the mixture with a fork, then mix in the bacon.

Spoon the yolk mixture into the cavities in the whites. Garnish with the pimento.

BAKED EGGS

Another way to cook eggs is by baking. It really is marvelously simple, disaster-proof, and practically fat-free. Here is a tasty recipe to start you off.

4. TANGY BAKED BAGEL EGGS

- 3 tablespoons butter or margarine
- 3 bagels, cut in half
- 6 eggs
- ½ teaspoon curry powder
- 3 teaspoons seasoned salt
- 1 teaspoon dill
- 3 teaspoons prepared mustard

Preheat the oven to 350°F.

Grease the baking dish with butter. Mix the curry powder into the mustard and spread it on the cut side of the bagels. Place the bagels cut side down in the baking dish. Carefully break an egg into the hole in each bagel. (Do not allow broken yolks to drop in; save them for scrambled eggs or cakes.) Sprinkle the dill and seasoned salt over the preparation.

Bake for 15 to 20 minutes or until the whites are *just* set.

The curious thing is that in this recipe the temperature is much higher (350°F) than for boiling (212°F) and the cooking time is longer than for hard-cooked egg, but the yolk remains semiliquid.

Winter hikers will understand this right away. You can tramp around in subzero weather for a good long time without chilling yourself. But if you have the misfortune to fall through ice into a pond of bitterly cold water, your survival time before you freeze to death is measured in minutes. You must get out, remove the wet clothes, and find warm shelter immediately.

This phenomenon is caused by the greater efficiency of liquids in moving heat around compared to air. Water is about a thousand times denser than air, and each molecule is ready to bear off its little portion of heat. The struggling hiker in the pond is having heat sucked out of his body at a tremendous rate compared to his friends standing on shore, shouting encouragement.

So an egg baked in air will cook more slowly than one cooked in water. And this is true even if the air is more than a hundred degrees hotter than the water.

POACHED EGGS

But boiling eggs can hold our interest for only so long. On to a dish that has been downtrodden so long it must have an inferiority complex—poached eggs. Kids and invalids curl a lip at what they should regard as a treat, for poaching is one of the best ways to cook an egg without destroying its "eggy" taste.

But it is not easy to do. Poorly poached, an egg ends up looking like a monster with white tentacles reaching for the sides of the skillet. The correct idea is to *set* the egg white as fast as possible, in order to form a "skin" that holds the egg in one piece as it *cooks.* Turning up the heat will not speed up the cooking, however; it will merely produce violent bubbling, which tears the egg apart.

The way to make the egg proteins coagulate faster is to use the same device that seals cracks in hard-cooked eggs — add *salt and/or acid.*

5. POACHED EGGS
(serves two)

- 4 eggs
- □ 2 teaspoons salt
- □ 4 tablespoons lemon juice (vinegar can substitute)

Have the eggs at *room temperature.* Using a *shallow skillet,* add water until it is about an *inch deep,* then put in the *salt* and *lemon juice.* Heat until the liquid *just simmers* — there should be *no big bubbles.*

Break an egg into a *wet saucer.* Bring the saucer to the surface of the liquid in the skillet and *slide* the egg into it. Repeat for the other eggs. *Cover the skillet.*

Cook them slowly at the *simmering temperature* until the whites are firm and the egg can be handled. Lift them out of the liquid with a slotted spatula, drain them momentarily on a rack, trim the edges, and serve quickly.

If you have more than an inch of water, the yolk will fall through it like a depth charge, and if you don't use a skillet, the egg will need a parachute before it hits the water. Neither result will be pleasing to the eye.

The salt or acid that salvaged the cracked egg by making the cooking water superefficient does the same job here. You can make your own combination of salt and acid to suit your taste.

There are three other tricks: using a saucer to slide the eggs smoothly into the water; reducing the temperature to below boiling to prevent destruction of the fragile "skin"; and using room-temperature eggs, which heat up and "set" more quickly than ones snatched straight from the refrigerator.

There are many elegant, delicious, and simple dishes that use poached eggs as the major ingredient. Here's an example:

6. EGGS SITTING PRETTY

- 6 slices toast
- 6 tablespoons cream cheese
- 6 slices (about ½ pound) of smoked salmon
- 6 poached eggs
- 2 tablespoons chopped dill
- 6 teaspoons capers

Spread the cream cheese on the toast, then lay on the smoked salmon. Put the capers on the fish and cover with the poached eggs. Sprinkle with the dill.

FRIED EGGS

For those of you who have had enough of health and nourishment, who have no fears of heart attacks or early death, we'll raise your spirits by putting some fat and cholesterol on the plate. Let's fry up some eggs.

In my mind, it is only in a woebegone rural diner, shunned by other travelers, that one can find the True Fried Egg. Only there will the full range of undeserved indignities be heaped on this simple dish: yolks like yellow peanut butter, whites that could be used as retreads, a border of crust dark as an obituary notice. If we are going to crack open the good work of an overtaxed hen, at least something palatable should result.

The problem here is violent overcooking. Most often the grill is set to a ridiculously high temperature, because—presumably such cooks hate cooking—they want to get it over with as quickly as possible.

When an egg is overcooked, two bad things happen. The most important is that the egg proteins, which have started to unfold and link themselves together, are pushed farther and faster than they want to go. They link up at every possible site, and since the molecules are no longer free to slide by each other, they form a sticky, rubbery structure. The water molecules, which hang on the proteins like barnacles, are forced out of these positions and vaporized as steam, thus drying and toughening the white even more.

The other bad reaction makes a dark crust at the border. It is called a *browning reaction*, for the obvious reason that it turns things brown. The sugar in the egg white and the protein combine to make the dark crust, but they do this only at high temperature.

The reason eggs get overcooked at home is that the cook waits for the top of the white to set. Very few people like runny egg white, but if you set the heat too high trying to cook it, the bottom will be overdone before the top sets.

The solution is to route some of the heat to the top of the egg. Some uncaring cookbooks advise fryers to spoon some of the hot fat or butter over the egg. But these days all the smart people are dieting and cooking without fat in nonstick skillets. So when the egg is half done, put a tablespoon of water in the pan and immediately clap a lid over it. The captive vapor will steam-heat the upper surface while the bottom is being slowly fried. Result—a tender, nonrunny fried egg.

Actually, enough water is given off by the egg itself so that merely covering it at the outset will do the same job. But that way you miss the moment of noisy vaporization and hurried sealing, which allows you a few Walter Mitty-like daydreams of chefing it at the Ritz.

7. FRIED EGGS
(one serving)

1 tablespoon butter, margarine, or cooking oil (optional)
2 eggs
□ 1 tablespoon water
salt
pepper
parsley, chopped

Heat the fat in a skillet with a nonstick coating. Break the eggs into a wet saucer and slip them one at a time into the skillet. Reduce the heat a bit and cook until half done. *Put 1 tablespoon of water into the skillet and immediately cover with a tight-fitting lid.* Cook only one minute more, or until the white on top has set.

Season to taste with salt and pepper and garnish with chopped parsley.

As long as we're frying eggs, let's have some fun with an omelet.

8. UPSIDE-DOWN OMELET

12 eggs
1 teaspoon salt
1 teaspoon pepper
1 teaspoon dry mustard
½ teaspoon garlic powder
1 tablespoon oil
1 pound Chinese sausages (Sausage Meat, Recipes 36 and 37 on page 66, can substitute.)

Cut the Chinese sausages into ½-inch pieces and boil them for 10 minutes in enough water to cover. Drain the meat and sauté it in a frypan until it is well done.

Heat the oil in a large skillet with a nonstick coating. Beat the eggs with the salt, pepper, mustard, and garlic powder, and pour them into the hot skillet. When the bottom of the omelet has set, reduce the heat a bit and add the meat. Using a spatula, lift a portion of the rim of the omelet and tilt the skillet so that the liquid egg runs between the omelet and the pan. Continue doing this around the periphery of the omelet until there is just a bit of liquid remaining on the omelet's surface.

Slide the omelet onto a platter, *invert* the skillet over it, and prepare to turn the whole assembly upside down. Put one hand under the platter and squeeze the skillet on top of it, then turn it over. Remove the platter.

The omelet will now be back in the skillet but upside down. Cook for 1 minute more, slide it onto the same platter, cut in wedges and serve.

It would be delightful to be able to pass, with Cinderella-like social mobility, to that most elegantly aristocratic of all egg dishes, the soufflé. But I am going to hoard my long-secret soufflé recipes until after I've explained sauces, later in the *Decoder*. They are easy to prepare but unforgiving; one mistake with the egg-white foam, and it's all over. So a little practice is welcome, and a good first step is a mousse.

This is an undemanding introduction to a marvelously useful, versatile, low-calorie, and low-cholesterol cooking technique — the egg-white foam. It is the basis of a wide variety of delights — meringue, cake, hot and cold soufflé — and is a foolproof leavening agent.

In one way it is even better than the other leaveners, yeast and baking powder, because one look at your foam will tell you if it is going to do the job. When the foam is light, fluffy, and voluminous, you are in business. But if it is slack, watery, and of small volume, it will do no good as a leavening agent, and that will be the time to rethink your day's objectives.

The basic idea is to pack a lot of captive air into that egg-white foam and then use it in a soufflé to expand the entire structure as it bakes, or in a mousse to lighten the texture. But the foam has to be stable enough to last until the preparation sets, either by cooking or by chilling.

The most important principle is cleanliness. Fat and grease are great foam killers; a greasy beer glass means a short-lived head (on the beer), and likewise an oily bowl will prevent the egg whites from foaming. Plastic bowls are notorious for the strength with which grease adheres to them, so avoid them when foaming eggs. And don't forget about the ingredients. There is a traitor hidden right in the middle of this recipe, in the yolk. Egg yolk is about 35 percent fat, and less than 0.1 percent contamination of yolk in white will decrease the foam volume.

Here's a little experiment to convince you.

AUTODEMONSTRATION C

Put two egg whites in each of two (nonplastic) bowls of the same material. Whip up the whites in one of the bowls and estimate the foam volume in a measuring cup. Add three drops of egg yolk to the other bowl, whip for the same length of time — and measure the difference.

So, if you are a nervous sort, separate each white into a saucer, then transfer it to the bowl. That way you can mess them up only one at a time. And if, despite every precaution, some egg yolk does slip into the white, turn your prospective soufflé into scrambled eggs, and better luck next time.

The reason an egg-white foam can be created at all is that the proteins are being "cooked" by the beating. The beating pulls the proteins out of their normal balled configurations, elongates them, and allows them to begin to form a rudimentary structure. This structure should be elastic enough to enclose the mass of air and yet strong enough to support the weight of the added ingredients. Beating does almost the same sort of thing that heat does, only not carried so far. But overbeating, just a few too many revolutions, will allow bonding between the molecules to produce a stiff, inelastic, three-dimensional network closer to "heat-cooked" egg white than to foam. You will have a problem folding in the other ingredients, and the foam will not expand to give much leavening when heated.

If a plastic bowl is bad for the whipping job, what is good for it? Any glass or enamel bowl will do the job, but it may take a bit of effort. The best bet is a metal bowl — especially copper, which is particularly effective. Aluminum, however, is a bad choice for aesthetic reasons — the beater may remove enough aluminum from the bowl to give the foam a grayish tinge.

In the following recipe for apple mousse, only one ingredient is added to the egg whites before beating — cream of tartar. Cream of tartar is a weak acid; the proteins in egg white are weakly alkaline. The alkalinity carries an electrical charge with it, so the proteins are kept apart by their like electrical charges but attract water molecules to cluster around and protect them. When the cream of tartar is added to the egg white, the proteins are neutralized, and the water molecules, suddenly uninterested in the bland character of the uncharged protein, drop away. Now there is no electrical repulsion or protective water sheath, and the proteins are easily coagulated to form the foam.

The addition of acid stabilizers is best done with a dry ingredient such as cream of tartar, which does not change its concentration either in manufacture or storage and does not dilute the proteins, as lemon juice or vinegar would.

A way to save time and your arm (if you are using a whisk) is to have the eggs at room temperature. Cold eggs will not foam as easily as warm ones because of *surface tension*. Surface tension is a force that wants to minimize the surface area of the white. Just as a balloon has a natural tendency to squeeze out its air and collapse, so each cell in the foam compresses its air. We want to maximize the surface area and stretch the white to include as much air as possible.

Merely warming the eggs from refrigerator temperature to room temperature will decrease the surface tension enough to make the foam easier to form.

In the last stage of the recipe, we mix the foam into everything else. It is folded in with a spatula or wooden spoon to prevent rough handling and air loss. At this moment these air cells are not permanent, so a delicate touch is needed to prevent the foam from being crushed.

Enough said. Here's the mousse.

9. APPLE MOUSSE

(4 – 5 cups)

2 cups applesauce
⅛ teaspoon cinnamon
1 tablespoon honey
3 tablespoons cream
2 tablespoons chocolate syrup
□ 4 egg whites
□ ¼ teaspoon cream of tartar

Mix the first four ingredients.

In another bowl, which is *neither aluminum nor plastic,* beat the egg whites with the cream of tartar until stiff peaks are formed when the stationary beaters are withdrawn.

With a spatula or wooden spoon fold the whites into the applesauce mixture. *Transfer it gently* to serving dishes, cover tightly, and chill in the freezer.

CHAPTER 1: RÉSUMÉ

I. BOILED (HARD AND SOFT) AND CODDLED

DO: Use fresh eggs
Pinhole the shell
Start in cold water
Add salt or vinegar (or other acid)
Douse in a cold water wash after cooking

DON'T: Use old eggs
Start a cold egg in hot water
Overcook

II. BAKED

DO: Bake at 325 – 350° F.

DON'T: Bake at too high an oven temperature
Overbake

III. POACHED

DO: Use fresh eggs
Use salt and/or acid (citrus juice, vinegar) in the poaching water
Have the water only at a simmer
Use a shallow pan

DON'T: Use old eggs
Have the water boiling rapidly

IV. FRIED

DO: Use fresh eggs
Use moderate heat
"Steam" the top

DON'T: Use old eggs
Use high heat
Overcook the bottom waiting for the top to set

V. OMELET

DO: Start in a hot skillet, then reduce heat
Let the liquid run between the omelet and the pan
Invert or fold the omelet to finish it

DON'T: Use high heat throughout
Overcook the bottom waiting for the top to cook

VI: EGG-WHITE FOAM

DO: Use clean copper, steel, glass or ceramic bowls
Use clean utensils
Have the whites at room temperature
Allow no egg yolk in the unbeaten whites
Use cream of tartar
Fold in other ingredients gently

DON'T: Use plastic or aluminum bowls
Use fat-contaminated utensils (beaters or bowls)
Let *any* egg yolk drop into the whites
Overbeat

2

VEGETABLES: "EAT THEM; THEY'RE GOOD FOR YOU"

Cookbooks love vegetables; so do mothers, teachers, and nutritionists, who repeatedly broadcast the message of nutrition and strong bodies. But as often as not, the audience rejects vegetables as objects of human consumption.

Reasons? They're too bland, too soggy. They all taste the same or look awful. Or just plain *ugh*.

Cookbooks are inconsistent in their approach to vegetables. Some books advise readers to cover them with a lid, while others expressly forbid it. A few advocate the addition of baking soda, but most find this unnatural. And some recipes really have it in for vegetables, urging huge pots of boiling water, skillets sizzling with oil, hot-breathed ovens ready for baking, barbecues piled high with glowing coals — a culinary torture chamber ready to do in any vegetable unfortunate enough to get within cooking distance.

The cook's impulse is to give in to despondency, forget the whole project, and make salad.

But there are remedies to the vegetable dilemma. First, better cooking to reflect the natural taste and texture of the individual foods. And second, some attention to the colors of what is on the plate and how they combine. There are more ways to whet the human appetite than heavy exercise.

Vegetables should be interesting to eat — and to prepare. Start by taking a good look at their colors. Vegetables are extraordinary food-dye factories. We use the extracted natural tints for cake and cookie decoration, and commercial food processors routinely add them to their products. In your kitchen, colors can serve as guideposts to the correct cooking path, not only to guard nutrients and produce agreeable flavors and textures, but to preserve the natural color. For too often we ignore the lesson these plants offer us — color serves a function. Moreover we can use color like seasoning, to awaken appetite.

When I once unthinkingly served a main course of whitefish with cream sauce, cauliflower, and rice, my guests seemed ready to doze off onto their plates. But another dinner of whitefish with tomato sauce, baked green pepper, and rice was polished off with alacrity and high spirits. Orientals have long known that the visual appeal of food is as important as its taste.

COLOR TYPES

There are four types of dyes that vegetables produce to color themselves. The sturdiest of all are the *carotene* ("carrot-een") dyes, which are found (of course) in carrots and other yellow or orange fruits and vegetables: corn, pumpkin, sweet potato, winter squash, peaches, and citrus fruits. There are also the odd examples of reddish carotenes in apricots, persimmons, pink grapefruit, paprika, red pepper, and tomato. These dyes are tough. Insensitive to heat or acidity, they can be overcooked in any way for any time without much color degradation.

Chemically speaking they are rather dull, even inert. As if recognizing this themselves, carotenes often try to be beautiful. Although they are present in all green vegetables, and in green leaves on trees, they hide their colors beneath the second kind of dye, the dominant green *chlorophyll*. Only in fall, when the chlorophyll fades, do the long-lived carotenes show off their beautiful yellows, oranges, and reds.

Those vegetables colored by chlorophyll are the ones most prevalent in our diet: artichokes, asparagus, beet tops, broccoli, Brussels sprouts, cabbage, Chinese cabbage, celery, chard, chicory, collards, cress, dandelion greens, endive, escarole, eggplant, green beans, green peppers, kale, lima beans, mustard greens, okra, peas, sorrel, spinach, summer squash, turnip greens, and zucchini.

The third kind of dye, the *anthocyanins* ("anth-owe-sigh-a-ninns"), produces the beautiful reds and blues found in beets, red cabbage, red onions, and most berries, while the fourth, the *anthoxanthins* ("anth-owe-xan-thins"), produces the creamy whites of cauliflower, kohlrabi, onions, parsnips, rice, and white cabbage.

These last three kinds of dyes — chlorophyll (green), anthocyanin (blue and red), and anthoxanthin (white) — will perform very unusual (and usually unwelcome) color changes for us. Since green vegetables are so frequently on the menu, let's start with them and see how their chemistry and our cooking will interact.

GREEN VEGETABLES

Although chlorophyll is terrific for photosynthesis, it is troublesome in cooking, its color being sensitive not only to the acidity of the cooking water and the heat applied, and but also to the acids contained *within* the vegetable as part of its cell composition. It is a rare molecule indeed that can change its structure without simultaneously changing color. Chlorophyll is no exception. It is held together by a magnesium atom, which rests at the hub of this complicated organic molecule. Acids, even the weak ones found within the plants themselves, can rip out the magnesium, collapsing the entire molecule and forming olive-brown or pale green molecular debris. If the vegetable has carotenes as well, a bronze-green hue may result. In any event the colors are real appetite quenchers. To see an example, try this:

AUTODEMONSTRATION D

2 cups raw green beans, cut up, or
2 cups chopped raw spinach
3½ cups water (2 cups in one pot, 1½ cups in the other)
½ cup vinegar

Bring the water to a boil in the two pots. Add the vinegar to the pot containing 1½ cups water. Add 1 cup of beans or spinach to each pot. Cook the beans 10 minutes; the spinach, 5.

Drain the vegetables and compare the colors

So hot acids (like vinegar) can destroy the chlorophyll, and so can the internal enemy: many vegetables contain acids within their cells. Once the cell membranes are altered during cooking the cellular plant acids are liberated and attack the dye.

But this chlorophyll, so central to the life of plant and man, is doubly vulnerable: alkalies will ruin it as well, turning the cooking water an extremely unpleasant color. (The vegetable won't look too good either.)

Autodemonstration D showed what happens when water is too acid for proper vegetable cooking. The next experiment examines the other side of the coin — tap water that is too alkaline.

AUTODEMONSTRATION E

- 2 cups green beans, cut up, or
- 2 cups Chinese cabbage, cut up
- 2 quarts water (1 quart in each of 2 pots)
- 1½ teaspoons bicarbonate of soda (baking soda)

Bring both pots of water to a boil. Add the baking soda to one of the pots. Put a cup of vegetables in each pot. Cook the beans 10 minutes, the cabbage 5.

Drain the vegetables and compare the colors and textures.

People accustomed to permanently maladjusted color TV might be able to fork the stuff down, but the alkaline baking soda wrecks the vegetables' cell walls while doing its color trick, and the food becomes too mushy to hold on a fork.

So we have to navigate between the hard rocks of acidity and alkalinity.* How will the cookbooks have us steer safely clear?

Some of them tell us to keep the pot lid off to allow the volatile acids to escape — a good idea, but you have to keep your eye on the water level and be immune to kitchen odors. Another way to reduce the plant-acid effect is to use a *lot* of cooking water; the more water around the vegetable, the more dilute the dissolved acid.

But the best idea for better vegetable taste and texture is to cook them *as little as possible*. Time is the close ally of acid and alkali. Try to do vegetables a bit underdone rather then overcooked. This is the natural route to experiencing their tastes and textures.

If you have a large bulky object to cook, like cabbage or eggplant, you can save a lot of cooking time by cutting up the vegetables. It will

(*If you do not know whether your tap water is acid or alkaline, it may not be easy to find out. The best way is probably to get on the phone to the local water department and ask for the lowdown. The only rule of thumb that seems to work is that very hard water tends to be alkaline.)

also mean a more uniform result. When a large vegetable is cooked whole, there is no way to avoid an overcooked exterior unless the center is underdone.

That large pot of cooking water will also help shorten cooking times. The idea is to keep the water temperature from falling too much when the raw vegetables, much cooler than the boiling water, are added. The more water, the smaller temperature dip as the food is dropped in, the less time to resume boiling, and the shorter the cooking time. Once the vegetables are in, keep the heat on high until the water returns to boiling, then turn it down. All we want to do is boil the water, not steam the kitchen.

There is a trick called *blanching* to halt the cooking instantaneously. The vegetables are removed from the boiling water and immediately plunged into cold water. This is great for foods to be served cold or to be stored and reheated.

10. ASPARAGUS VINAIGRETTE

- 3 pounds young asparagus
- □ boiling water in a *large* pot
- 2 tablespoons wine vinegar
- 1 tablespoon lemon juice
- 1 teaspoon prepared mustard
- ½ teaspoon salt
- ¼ teaspoon pepper
- ¼ teaspoon garlic powder
- ½ teaspoon chives
- ½ teaspoon parsley
- 8 tablespoons olive oil

Snap off and discard the tough ends of the asparagus. Add the head ends to the boiling water. Cook for 12 to 15 minutes, or until *just* tender. Drain immediately and immerse the asparagus in a pot of cold water until cool. Drain well. Refrigerate if necessary.

Put the remaining ingredients (reserving 2 tablespoons of olive oil) in a blender and blend at high speed for 5 seconds. Add the remaining oil, if desired, to taste.

Serve the asparagus with the dressing on the side so even your dieting friends can enjoy it.

Of course, it would be simple to cut down on cooking time if it were done at a higher temperature. But that is easier said than done, since a liquid cannot be heated hotter than its boiling point.

"Boiling" means that the bubbles of vapor rising in the liquid have an internal pressure the same as the air around us. So, when they pop, the moisture inside them (steam) escapes from the confining liquid into the air. Turning up the heat makes more bubbles and boils away the liquid *faster,* but does not raise it to a *higher temperature.*

The only practical way to change the boiling point is to change the air pressure. Nature does this for us, providing low air pressure during stormy weather and high pressure during fair weather. At low pressure, for example, the liquid boils when the bubbles have an internal pressure equal to the air pressure, and since this is low, so is the temperature needed to produce it. Low pressure, low boiling point. High pressure, high boiling point.

But few cooks can wait around for the weatherman to accommodate them. And the change in the boiling point is so small as to make it useless for our purposes.

One way to get really low boiling points is by going up into the mountains. In Salt Lake City, 5,000 feet above sea level, the boiling point is down to 203°F, and in Aspen, Colorado, at 8,000 feet, the boiling point is only 198°F. The greater the altitude, the thinner the air and the lower its pressure. As the atmospheric pressure pushing down on the water is reduced, it becomes easier to expel the bubbles of steam from the liquid, so it can happen at this much reduced temperature.

When the ski-bum waiter at the Eagle's Nest Restaurant at the top of a ski lift at 11,000 feet brings you a cup of coffee that is not as warming as its price tag, it is not the waiter's fault. Water simply will not boil above 198°F at that altitude.

To counteract the low pressure, high-altitude cooks resort to the pressure cooker. So useful is this device, in fact, that Indian foot soldier in the Himalayas are issued portable pressure cookers as standard equipment.

Just as high altitude causes water to boil at a *lower* temperature than at sea level, so a pressure cooker causes it to boil at a *higher* temperature — by doubling the normal air pressure.

The bubbles of water vapor in a pressure cooker can escape from the liquid only at this doubly high pressure, so the pressure within the bubble and the temperature must be commensurately higher. The boiling point in the pressure cooker has been cranked up to 250°F.

This may not seem like an enormous change to you, but biochemical molecules are as heat sensitive as fair-skinned sunbathers their first day at the beach. At 250°F molecules will rearrange about ten times faster than at 212°F. Whole asparagus, while normally boiled for 10 to 15 minutes, requires only 1 to 2 minutes in a pressure cooker.

Other time savings are similarly dramatic: for broccoli, 8 to 20 minutes versus ½ to 1½ minutes; for turnips, 10 to 20 minutes versus 1½ to 3 minutes. Cooking time is cut down by about a factor of ten.

Pressure cooking is an excellent technique for vegetables because they cook for such a short time. This gentle treatment yields better-tasting food, saves fuel, and saves time in the kitchen. But there are some pitfalls to pressure cookery, closely associated with these virtues. When the cooking time is refined down to half minutes, it is easy to err and thereby overcook—just what we are trying to avoid. *So one must be very careful with the timing.*

If you think this is too much trouble and a pressure cooker too heavy to push around a stove, try cooking vegetables out of water. If you can manage to lift the food an inch or two above the water surface, it will cook by steaming.

Steaming is a lovely technique for the vegetables and a lot of fun for the cook. It is certainly not a very fast method, but it makes overcooking almost impossible. And if your water is too alkaline for cooking properly, it solves that problem too.

When you are steaming food, you are running a small still. Like any other distillation, this one results in a purification. The non-volatile acid or alkali elements are left behind in the liquid as the water vaporizes. As it condenses on the food, it is in a pure form. The worse the condition of your water, the better does steaming seem as a cooking choice.

If you are lucky enough to live in a town with a Chinese grocery store, you can buy excellent and inexpensive stackable bamboo

steamers. The stackable feature gives you a lot of versatility. Suppose you want to steam three items, but they require different cooking times—say 5, 10, and 20 minutes. Just steam the last one for 10 minutes, then stack the next one on and cover it, and 5 minutes later stack on and cover the last. Five minutes later you are ready to serve a perfectly cooked dinner of three items, and you have had only one burner or element going on your stove.

In addition to these Oriental devices, metal steamers are available in most housewares departments, and if you don't want to go to the expense of buying a special pot, a little ingenuity will turn a colander, strainer, or french-fried-potato drainer, suspended inside a large covered saucepan, into a serviceable unit. Try out this recipe:

11. STEAMED CHICKEN, SAUSAGE, AND BROCCOLI

- 4–5 pounds of chicken, cut in small pieces
- 3 tablespoons sherry
- 1 tablespoon cornstarch
- 2 green onions, minced
- 2 slices ginger, minced
- 1 teaspoon salt
- ½ teaspoon garlic powder
- 1 pound Chinese sausages (Italian sausages can substitute)
- 1 bunch broccoli, cut in flowerets
- ½ cup soy sauce
- 1½ teaspoons sesame oil

Brush the chicken with a mixture of sherry, cornstarch, green onions, ginger, salt, and garlic. Let stand in the refrigerator for at least an hour.

Soak the sausages in warm water for 5 to 10 minutes to soften them. Cut them into ½-inch lengths (smaller if you are using the larger Italian kind).

Put the chicken and sausages in the steamer, cover and steam for 30 minutes. Add another bamboo steamer rack containing the broccoli. (If you are using a single steamer, just uncover, add the broccoli, and re-cover.) Continue steaming for another 15 minutes.

Simmer the soy sauce and sesame oil in a saucepan. Serve the chicken, sausage, and broccoli with the soy/sesame as a side dish.

Cooking at even higher temperatures means getting away from water-based cookery and progressing to baking and frying. Baking is analogous to steaming in that hot gas transfers much of the heat;

frying is analogous to boiling, because the food is immersed in a liquid. But both are carried out in the absence of water and do not present any acid/alkali hazard to the food.

We will check out the detailed science of these two techniques in subsequent chapters, but for the moment it is sufficient to realize that baking is fairly quick and frying is very quick,and that the absence of water *ipso facto* eliminates most of those troubles we have been talking about.

Baking is best done dry. If you try to do it in too small an oven or casserole, the vapor given off by the food itself will start to stew things. One of the reasons barbecued food tastes so good is that none of the steam can recondense on the food; it is an absolutely dry cooking technique. (If it doesn't rain.)

Frying is also best done dry. Any water present in the fat just cools it off and soaks up energy as it vaporizes. So one trick is to dry off the vegetables carefully before adding them to the hot fat or oil.

12. EGGPLANT PIZZAIOLA

1 eggplant
½ cup (approx.) oil for frying
6 ounces sliced mozzarella cheese
2 small (1¾ ounce/50 grams size) cans anchovies, drained
2 teaspoons oregano
¼ teaspoon salt
¼ teaspoon pepper

Peel the eggplant and cut it into ½-inch slices. Soak the slices in a bowl of warm water for 15 minutes, then *drain and dry them carefully with paper towels.*

Heat the oil in a skillet and fry the eggplant, one or two slices at a time, until they turn brown. Remove them to a greased baking dish, cover each with a slice of cheese and two anchovy strips in a cross. Sprinkle the seasonings over them and heat under the broiler (or salamander) until the cheese melts.

Serve as an appetizer.

The soaking gets rid of some of the bitter taste of raw eggplant, which luckily happens to be water soluble. The subsequent careful drying eliminates the last vestiges of moisture, ensuring a high frying temperature and a nice crisp exterior.

The other trick for keeping things dry is to soak up the surface moisture with flour or breading. These coatings will also insulate the surface and keep it from scorching and may even help hold delicate foods in one piece.

13. FRIED GREENERY

4 zucchini	¼ cup cornstarch
3 green peppers	1 cup water
¼ pound green beans	2 teaspoons salt
1 cup flour	1 teaspoon sugar
1 teaspoon baking powder	1 teaspoon oil

Heat a deep fryer to 360 to 380°F.

Cut the zucchini into ¼-inch-thick slices, the pepper into ¼-inch strips, and snip off the ends of the green beans and cut them in 1-inch lengths. *Dry everything thoroughly with paper towels.*

Make a batter of the other ingredients by mixing them thoroughly until there are no large lumps. (The batter should be thick.)

Dip the dry vegetables into the batter so they are completely coated. Deep-fry them until they are browned. Drain the cooked pieces on paper towels and serve immediately.

A few words of warning to novice deep-fryers. Be careful! Hot oil is deceptively dangerous. It does not boil, so there is no immediate visual warning of its temperature. Always regard it with suspicion.

When hot it is very flammable, and an oil fire is a real danger if treated in the normal way — that is, by throwing some water on it. Oil and water do *not* mix — old sayings are often right — and the water will just scatter the oil and spread the fire around. To deal with an oil fire in the pot, cover the pot with a lid, which will cut off the supply of oxygen and quickly douse the flames. If the burning oil has spilled on the floor or other surfaces, cover it with a good handful or two of salt or baking soda (bicarbonate of soda). Baking soda is particularly effective, because it not only smothers the oil and cuts off the oxygen, but when hot it releases carbon dioxide and thus acts like a tiny CO_2 fire extinguisher. (So does baking powder.)

But please do not think that almost any dry foodstuffs will do. Sugar works once in a while, but most of the time it simply burns. (That's how caramel is made — by burning sugar.) Rice, beans, and similar substances are not fine-grained enough to smother the

flames. And flour is most definitely *not* recommended. Flour explodes. Flour mills are always in danger of blowing up. So are kitchens, and even a petite-sized explosion can set adjoining rooms — and you — on fire.

To sum up: If the fire is in a container, use a large lid. If it has also spilled over the pot onto the burner or heating elements, *do not remove the pot*. Put a lid on it, and use a lot of salt or bicarbonate of soda in the space between the utensil and the burner. (If you lift the pot, there is more air for the fire to feed on and more opportunity for the flames to set something else alight.) If the flames are on working surfaces, walls, or floors, use the salt or bicarb liberally. *Do not use water on an oil fire.*

But the best defense is an ABC-type fire extinguisher, which handles all kinds of home fires and is effective at a 20-foot range. Give one as a wedding gift.

STIR-FRY

The Oriental cooking technique called stir-fry combines two of the best ideas for vegetable cookery: fast-frying and steaming. The food is cut up fine, usually in julienne strips, and quickly sautéed, bit by bit. Then everything is returned to the sauté pan, which is promptly covered so the foods will be steamed to finish their cooking. It is all the rage; give it a try.

TABLE I
Green Vegetables

Technique	*Temperature*	*Time*	*Acid/Alkali Hazard?*	*Preservation of Vitamins, Taste & Texture*
Boiling*	212°F	Short	Yes	Undercook
Pressure Cooking	250°F	Very short	Yes	Undercook
Steaming	212°F	Medium	No	Undercook
Baking	300–400°F	Medium	No	Undercook
Frying+	325–400°F	Very short	No	Undercook

*Use lots of boiling water; cut up the vegetable.
+Dry the vegetables before frying. Use flour or breading for further drying before frying.

RED-BLUE VEGETABLES

The two remaining color classes, red-blues and whites, have very special properties. The beautiful red and blue vegetables that contain anthocyanins (beets, red cabbage, red onions) will show extraordinary color changes as the acidity varies.

Check it out for yourself.

AUTODEMONSTRATION F

2 cups *red* cabbage, shredded
4 cups water (2 cups in each of two pots)
½ cup vinegar
1 teaspoon bicarbonate of soda (baking soda)

Boil the water in the first pot and add 1 cup of cabbage and 1 tablespoon of vinegar. Continue boiling. The cabbage will turn reassuringly red.

Now boil the water in the second pot, add the other cup of raw cabbage and the bicarbonate of soda, bit by bit. The cabbage will turn purple, red-blue or blue. Now add the rest of the vinegar (the water will foam), and see the color change reverse itself to red.

So these red-blue pigments are acid/alkali-dependent, and they are soluble in water. If they weren't soluble, borscht might be as colorless as vodka. So when making beet soup, we take advantage of this and make the color as intense as possible by cutting the beets into little pieces so the dye can be more effectively leached into the soup water.

14. RUTH'S BORSCHT

- 2 pounds beets (2 quarts), peeled and *grated*
- 2 quarts beef bouillon
- 2 onions, quartered
- 1 can (5½ ounce/156 milliliters) tomato paste
- 1 tablespoon sugar
- 1 – 2 teaspoons salt
- 1 teaspoon pepper
- 1 teaspoon grated lemon rind
- 6 boiled peeled potatoes, or
- 6 hard-cooked eggs, shelled, or ½ cup sour cream

Simmer all the ingredients, except the last three, in a heavy kettle for 1 hour.

Serve hot or cold with boiled peeled potatoes and/or hard-cooked eggs and/or sour cream.

[*Note:* The lemon is added as rind, to get the flavor without the acidity, which would turn the soup a paler red.]

But now if we want to boil beets for their own sakes, we must keep the color in the vegetable by cooking them whole in their skins and cutting them up when they are out of the water. If you have a vibrant color, flaunt it!

15. BABY BEET SALAD

(four servings)

- □18 small beets, washed and trimmed, but with 1 inch of stalks left on
- 2 quarts water
- ½ cup (125 milliliters) sour cream
- 1 tablespoon honey
- 1 teaspoon lemon juice

Boil the beets, *covered*, in the water until they are tender (60 to 90 minutes). For a cooking period this long, use a lid, so you won't have to replenish the cooking water too often. (Steaming will take about 10 to 15 minutes longer and pressure cooking will take just 15 minutes — or less — of cooking time.)

Discard the cooking water. Slip off and discard the skins of the beets. Dice the beets and chill them.

Combine the other ingredients and add to the beets.

As we saw in Autodemonstration F, these red-blue vegetables are better off in acid, avoiding the texture and dye breakdown that alkalies produce. Cooks around the world knew this long before chemists ever developed the concept of acidity. Universally, they combined these vegetables with *acidic foodstuffs* to guard their color. The following recipes show how inventive cooks conformed to this chemical principle.

16. BOILED RED CABBAGE

- 12 strips bacon
- □ 1 *red* cabbage, shredded
- 2 onions, sliced
- 2 quarts water
- 2 teaspoons salt
- □ ¼ cup lemon juice
- 1 tablespoon sugar
- □ 1 tablespoon wine vinegar
- ½ teaspoon pepper
- 1½ tablespoons caraway seeds

Cook the bacon in a frying pan until it is very well done. Dry it on paper towels. Reserve 4 tablespoons of the drippings and discard the rest.

Cook the cabbage and onions in boiling water to which 1 teaspoon of salt and the lemon juice have been added. When the vegetables are *barely tender* (5 to 10 minutes), drain them thoroughly.

Reheat the reserved bacon drippings in the frying pan, stir in the other ingredients (including the second teaspoon of salt), the vegetables, and the bacon after you have crumbled it.

Cook 10 minutes more.

17. BAKED RED CABBAGE

- □ 1 *red* cabbage, shredded
- 2 onions, diced
- 1 pound pepperoni, diced
- □ 3 cups sour cream
- □ ½ small can (6¼ fluid ounces/ 178 milliliter size) frozen orange juice, thawed
- 2 tablespoons oil
- □ 2 tablespoons honey
- 1 teaspoon salt
- ½ teaspoon pepper

Preheat the oven to 350°F.

Sauté the onion and pepperoni in the oil until the onions are golden and the pepperoni is brown. Mix them with all the other ingredients, except 1½ cups of the sour cream, and transfer to a casserole. Cover and bake for 1¼ to 1½ hours, or until the cabbage is tender. If there is excess liquid, uncover the casserole and stir a bit during the baking.

Mix in the remaining 1½ cups of sour cream and serve.

These recipes have a common thread, different ingredients that perform the same function — maintaining the red color and good texture of the cabbage. In each recipe the acid ingredients which do this are indicated with our famous square □: lemon juice, vinegar, sour cream, citrus juice, and honey. When you concoct your own red cabbage (or red onion or beet) recipe, just put in a tart ingredient like one of these, or dry wine, cider, fruit jelly, etc. Then you know that you are free to add whatever else your imagination leads you to.

WHITE VEGETABLES

The last class of dyes are the creamy white anthoxanthins. Like the red-blue dyes, they are better off in acidic surroundings. If alkali gets to them for too long, they will turn yellow.

They can react with iron from a pot or knife or a chipped enameled utensil, causing a dark discoloration, usually blue-green or brown.

They can react even with aluminum to give bright yellow or brown colors. So avoid iron and aluminum containers and utensils when cooking these items.

A few other vegetables, such as asparagus and sweet potato, will discolor in the presence of iron because they are high in tannins (substances that make strong tea taste astringent). Vinegar also has a lot of tannin, so avoid ironware when cooking dishes like Recipe 16, Boiled Red Cabbage (p. 32).

TABLE II

Red-blue and White Vegetables

Technique	*Alkaline hazard? Red-blue and White*		*Iron/Aluminum hazard? Red-blue*	*White*
Boiling*	Yes	Use an acid ingredient in the recipe (unless you *want* a dark color, say for borscht)	Iron only	Both iron and aluminum
Pressure Cooking	Yes			
Steaming	No			
Baking	No			
Frying†	No			

*Acidify the cooking water; use lots of boiling water; cut up the vegetables.
†Dry the vegetables before frying. Use flour or breading for further drying before frying.

VITAMINS

Even very good food can be drastically reduced in nutritional content by unthinking cooking. Every now and then it's wise to remember this.

Of course, vitamin-loss-when-cooking-vegetables is one of the great old themes of government literature. Born in wartime out of food-shortage worries, these phantom pamphlets continue to haunt us through every crisis. But the propaganda, tiresome or not, happens to be correct. Why shouldn't we get as much nutrition as we can from our food dollar?

The vitamin scene is very simple, yet terribly complicated. First, the simple matters.

The B family of vitamins and vitamin C are all water soluble. So vegetables lose these nutrients to the cooking water when we boil, pressure-cook, or steam them — especially if they have been cut up. Of these techniques, simple boiling loses the most, so it is best to avoid if you are worried about your vitamin ration when cooking foods rich in B and C.

Vitamin B family:	Green leafy vegetables (spinach, collards, dandelion greens, kale, mustard greens, turnip greens), broccoli, Brussels sprouts, cabbage, cauliflower, kohlrabi, okra, potato, and legumes (peas, lima beans, soybeans, lentils, kidney beans, navy beans) Nonvegetable sources are cereal grains, enriched bread, and milk and cheese
Vitamin C:	Spinach, collards, broccoli, cabbage, peppers, tomato, and potato Nonvegetable sources are citrus fruits, apples, melons, and strawberries

Vitamins A and D, on the other hand, are not water soluble. They are fat soluble and are relatively resistant to whatever we do to them in the kitchen.

Vitamin A:	Green leafy and yellow-orange vegetables (carrots, corn, pumpkin, sweet potato, and winter squash) Nonvegetable sources are butter, eggs, milk and fish liver
Vitamin D:	Vegetables are not an important source of this vitamin Nonvegetable sources are mostly fat fish (herring, mackerel, salmon, sardine) and fortified milk

So it is really only the B family and C that need concern us, but they are doubly difficult, for not only will they be leached out by the cooking water, but some — especially C — will be destroyed by oxygen in the air if the temperature is high enough. If you mash or blend a hot potato, for example, the air will have a lot of opportunity to get at Vitamin C and destroy up to 50 percent of it.

A true vitamin conservationist will cook vegetables unpared (many vitamins lie just under the skin), as fresh as possible, and will eat them up right away.

Table III
Vitamins

Vitamins:	*A*	*D*	*B family*	*C*
Soluble	Fat		Water	
Loss to cooking water?	Little		Yes!	
Loss on heating?	Little		Yes!	
Recommendations	Do as you please		Cook quickly; serve immediately; use cooking water for soup or sauce	
Vegetable containing it	Green leafy and Yellow/orange	Little	Green leafy, broccoli, cabbage, potato	Legumes, pepper, tomato

Finally, what don't we know? About individual nutritional and vitamin needs — let alone their interaction with protein, carbohydrate, fat, and minerals — a vastness. And when we add to the equation the combination of cooking time and temperatures, plus the extent of slicing, the amount of cooking water, its alkalinity, and the storage and growing history of the vegetable, only an oracle would give a clear-cut answer.

I am no oracle, but I'll still attempt an answer: Be fast! Get it in! Get it out! Serve it up!

CHAPTER 2: RÉSUMÉ

I. COLOR TYPES

A. Yellow (carotene): Carrots, corn, pumpkins, sweet potatoes, winter squash
Nonvegetable: peaches and citrus fruits

B. Green (chlorophyll): Artichoke, asparagus, broccoli, Brussels sprouts, green (summer) cabbage, Chinese cabbage, celery, chard, chicory, collards, cress, dandelion greens, endive, escarole, eggplant, green beans, green pepper, kale, okra, lima beans, peas, sorrel, spinach, summer squash, zucchini

C. Red-blue (anthocyanin): Beets, red cabbage, and red onions
Nonvegetable: most berries

D. White (anthoxanthin): White cabbage, cauliflower, kohlrabi, onion, parsnips, rice

II. GREEN VEGETABLES (See *Table I, page 30)*

DO:
- Undercook
- Use lots of water when boiling
- Cut up the vegetable (if possible) when boiling
- Blanch vegetables to be refrigerated after boiling
- Ventilate when baking
- Dry the vegetable thoroughly before frying

DON'T:
- Overcook
- Use bicarbonate unless your cooking water is *very* acidic
- Mistime when using a pressure cooker
- Fry in oil that is not hot enough

III. RED-BLUE AND WHITE VEGETABLES (See *Table II, page 34)*

DO:
- As for Green Vegetables, but
- Use an acid ingredient when boiling or pressure cooking

DON'T:
- Same as for Green Vegetables, but in addition, don't
- Use iron cookware or utensils with red-blue vegetables
- Use iron or aluminum cookware or utensils with white vegetables.

IV. YELLOW VEGETABLES

DO: As you please!

V. VITAMINS (See *Table III, page 36)*

DO:
- Cook the vegetables quickly
- Serve them quickly
- Use fresh produce (if possible)
- Use cooking water for soup or sauce

DON'T:
- Overcook
- Overpeel

3

GARLIC, ONIONS, CABBAGE, AND POTATOES: VAMPIRE REPELLENTS AND UNLIKELY APHRODISIACS

GARLIC AND ONIONS

The emotional content of garlic almost equals its culinary value. American fathers may be driven apoplectic if a daughter's suitor has too much garlic on his breath. On the other hand, Mediterranean fathers would lose interest in life and food if the garlic supplies were suddenly to run out. The most honored place in Transylvania cuisine (at least the Hollywood version) is reserved for garlic, the Vampire Repellent. For the rest of us, the idea is to use it tactfully to season the food and not the hands and house.

Actually, as a food garlic is itself a bit neurotic and unstable, constantly on the brink of self-destruction. Garlic possesses within itself a chemical, *alliin* ("a-lean"), and an enzyme, *alliinase* ("a-lean-ace"). Whenever these two are put in contact, the enzyme will destroy the alliin, pulling it apart and by this act producing "garlic flavor." But this reaction is held in abeyance by a cell membrane, which separates the two. Only when we interfere and remove this membrane barrier can the reaction proceed. This means that we can control garlic flavor. It will develop in response to what we do to the cell membranes.

The principal molecular product responsible for garlic flavor is a sulfur compound, larger and more complicated (but less obnoxious) than the hydrogen sulfide of rotten eggs. Onions, chives, and leeks, first cousins of garlic, have flavors caused by similar sulfur-bearing molecules. This chemical group is extremely potent, as our noses can tell us. Even an average untrained nose will wrinkle at sulfide concentrations of 1 part in 3 million.

But these are the flavor molecules. They are not the ones responsible for our tears when cutting onions. However, the chemical scenarios for the production of these different agents are identical. A molecule and an enzyme that can decompose it are separated by a cell membrane. When we cut the onion, the two are put in contact, and *another* sulfur-containing molecule is generated. Our tear ducts start to work immediately.

But this particular molecule is quite different from the flavor molecules in one regard, and this provides us with a defense. It turns out that the molecule is water soluble, and if you cut an onion under running water, these molecules will dissolve and be washed away before they get near your eyes.

There is a folk belief that clenching a half-burned wooden match between the teeth is also an effective tear-preventive. This is unlikely. Holding this posture as you work does put a small stick of charcoal right there under your nose, and charcoal is a good gas absorber. But unless you have a reserve of *well-aged* burned matches salted away, the unpleasant smell of recent combustion will merely

substitute for the food odors. Your best bet is to use water, a food processor, one of those enclosed-glass chopping devices, or a pair of plastic protective goggles lifted from the family workshop.

So here are these two enzyme reactions — one producing flavor and the other tears. We can deal with the latter easily enough as we have seen, but how can we control the garlic intensity? The best way is to limit the amount of cutting and mincing of the garlic bulb. For once the knife cuts the cell membrane and allows alliin to contact alliinase, the reaction is instantaneous. All you can do is regulate how much of them are allowed to contact each other.

Enzyme reactions are unusual in that they are very rapid and do not benefit from heat to make them faster. Anyone who has cooked pasta, sauces, vegetables, roasts, bread — whatever — knows it takes time and heat. But garlic flavor develops as quickly as the knife passes through the bulb. Why is it so fast? What happens after the membrane is cut, and the alliin finds the alliinase?

Alliin has a weak link in its structure — weak, but not totally enfeebled, so normally it can hold itself together. But the close contact with the enzyme forces it into a new position, which puts a strain on the weak link. Just as a movie projector forces a flexible film to follow its curved guides and rollers, so the enzyme forces the molecule into a new and unaccustomed posture. This opens it up, exposing and straining the weak link, and rendering it easy to break.

Once that weak link, the chemical bond, is broken and new garlic-flavored molecules are formed, the enzyme releases its hold, freeing them to find their way to our noses and palates. The next alliin molecule takes its place on top of the enzyme, and the identical sequence is played out.

Our normal way of forcing reactions in the kitchen is to heat them up. We cook the food. But in this case it is the enzyme that does the

WHAT HAPPENS WHEN YOU CUT A GARLIC:

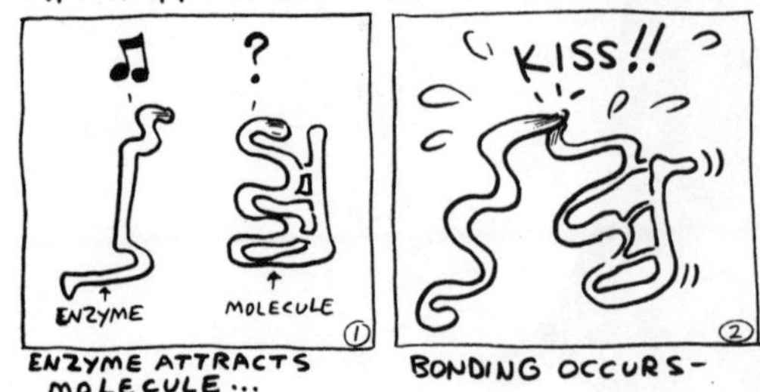

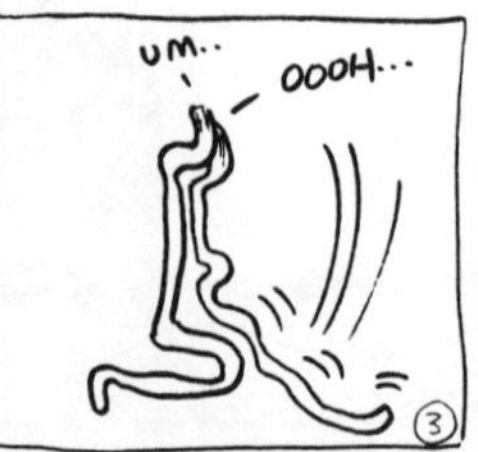

MMMMM
AHHH
BLUB BLUB
H
O
H
EXPOSED TO WATER MOLECUL

Figure 5. Enzyme-catalyzed reaction.

forcing. So the odor of garlic or the tear-inducing factor of onions is not already there in the vegetable waiting to be let out. It is manufactured on the spot whenever we break the cell-membrane barrier by slicing, crushing, mincing, or mushing.

It is easy to use this idea to throttle the amount of flavor these items add to our preparations. Just match the amount of membrane destruction — the enthusiasm with which you go after the garlic clove with your knife or how thoroughly you mash it — with how much garlic taste you want in the food.

To start you off, here's a recipe where the garlic never gets cooked at all:

18. GREEK CUCUMBER SALAD

3 cucumbers, peeled
2 small onions, thinly sliced
2 cups (500 milliliters) sour cream
□ 2 cloves garlic, *minced*
□ 1 tablespoon salt
1 tablespoon olive oil
1 tablespoon lemon juice
2 dozen black olives

Grate the cucumbers, drain them, and press them and the sliced onions between absorbent paper towels.

Mash the garlic with the salt and combine it with the other ingredients. The salt acts as an abrasive on the garlic.

Another way to modify garlic flavor is by cooking it. As it heats up, the membranes are gradually destroyed, permitting the enzyme reactions to proceed. Since these processes take place gradually and

WATER MOLECULE ATTACKS.

A SPLIT IS CREATED.

THEY MOVE TO AN UNSPECTING NOSE..

CREATING A NASAL REACTION!

at a relatively high temperature, the result will taste somewhat different from flavor released by cutting. You can even make a soup out of garlic with this technique. The taste intensity is reduced by not cutting the clove at all.

19. GARLIC SOUP

- □ 10 to 20 cloves garlic, peeled *but not cut**
- 2 tablespoons olive oil
- 6 cups chicken stock
- ½ teaspoon salt
- ½ teaspoon pepper
- 1 tablespoon parsley, chopped
- ¼ cup mayonnaise
- 12 rounds of toast, warmed
- 6 tablespoons Parmesan cheese

Sauté the garlic cloves gently, *without bruising*, in the olive oil for 10 minutes. Transfer them to a soup pot and add the stock and seasonings. Cook for 30 minutes.

Discard the garlic cloves. Pour the soup into bowls, add the toast rounds (2 per bowl), and garnish with the Parmesan cheese.

The length of time these items are left to cook also influences the intensity of the flavors. These sulfides are relatively small, light molecules and ultimately vaporize away from the food. So here is another way of moderating garlic (or onion) flavor. Of course, you have to play a cautious game; if you cook it some but not enough, the membranes will soften, the enzyme reactions take place, and the flavors develop to a maximum, but the molecules will not have a chance to vaporize away. So, keep tasting until you are happy with the results.

To sum up, garlic and its relatives are controllable by knife and heat. The next Autodemonstration will determine how dedicated you are to culinary science.

*Boil the garlic for 1 or 2 minutes to facilitate the peeling.

AUTODEMONSTRATION G

- 3 cloves garlic
- 3 tablespoons oil

Carefully peel the garlic cloves without bruising or cutting them. (Do not use the 2-minute boiling trick either.) Heat the oil in a frying pan.

Mince two of the cloves and sauté one of them for 2–5 minutes, until it is browned. Drain it carefully.

Now give each sample, the whole clove, the minced raw clove, and the minced sautéed clove, a close olfactory inspection. Then, if possible, taste a small portion of each sample.

Well, I won't blame you for passing this one by, but they each give a different odor and taste, and you can tailor your recipe for whatever effect you desire.

STUFFING

There is one exception to the rule of cooking to taste, and it involves cooking something you can't get at *to* taste — namely, poultry stuffing. Stuffing is the last part ot the roast bird to feel the heat, and thus when the bird is done to a turn, the stuffing often is not. This is not only a culinary problem but a health one, since half-cooked stuffing may contain unkilled-off bacteria. Extreme caution and application of the rules of hygiene must be observed when preparing stuffing.

Cookbooks tacitly admit the problem of undercooked stuffing when they tell us to sauté (or boil) the onions before adding them to the mixture. If raw onions are used and then *undercooked*, their taste would overwhelm the other ingredients. The solution is to dice the onions and precook them. Since the onion pieces are small and the temperature high, most of the sulfide reactions are complete and the products vaporized away by the time the onions are golden. The moderate cooking that the stuffing later receives just blends the flavors.

20. ONION-LIVER-RICE STUFFING
(6 cups)

- □ 4 onions, chopped
- ⅛ pound butter
- ½ pound chicken livers, cut up
- ½ cup mushrooms, sliced
- 3 cups cooked white rice
- 4 tablespoons Marsala (or port) wine
- 1 teaspoon salt
- ½ teaspoon pepper
- ½ teaspoon oregano

Sauté the onions in butter until they are golden. Add the chicken livers and spices, cooking until tender. Add the mushrooms and wine and cook 5 minutes more, then remove from the heat and mix in with the rice.

Everything that must be *well* cooked must be *pre*cooked if it is used as a stuffing ingredient. Any ground meat, and *especially* pork, must get a good going-over at the outset.

21. SAUSAGE STUFFING
(7 cups)

- □ 3 onions, chopped
- □ ½ pound sausage meat (commercial or from Recipe 36 or 37)
- 2 tablespoons oil
- 3 apples, pared, cored, and sliced
- 1 tablespoon lemon juice
- 1 small can (10 ounces/284 milliliters) mandarin oranges, drained
- 1 teaspoon salt
- ½ teaspoon pepper
- ½ teaspoon paprika
- 3 cups fresh or stale bread, cubed

Heat the oil in a sauté pan and *sauté the onions* until they are golden. Remove the onion and *sauté the sausage meat until it is well done*. Discard as much of the grease as possible. Add the apple, lemon juice, oranges, and seasonings, and cook 15 minutes more, returning the onions to the pan during the last 5 minutes of cooking.

Mix in with the bread.

If you really want to be safe, cook stuffings *separately* from the bird. For these, bake in a casserole or wrapped in aluminum foil for about 30 minutes at 350°F.

CABBAGE

Cabbage and its cousins also tend to generate unwelcome smells in your kitchen if allowed. These are produced in the same way as in garlic and onion — by cutting a cell membrane to allow an enzyme to contact a reactive molecule.

Red or white cabbage, cauliflower, cress, bok choy, broccoli, brussels sprouts, kohlrabi, turnips, and mustard all contain compounds analagous to the one present in cabbage, *sinigrin*. When the cell walls are broken, an enzyme, *myrosinase* ("my-roe-sin-ace"), decomposes the sinigrin to mustard oil, the odor of raw shredded cabbage. After a while this compound breaks down to hydrogen sulfide, the bad actor of hard-boiled eggs, and other equally unpleasant compounds. So in cabbage-serving homes — traditionally in boardinghouses, where the food was left cooking until the last lodger arrived home — odors would be the order of the day.

As usual the best defense against cabbage smell is speedy cooking. Use a lot of water already at the boil, so that it will return to the boil quickly after the addition of the cabbage. Cook covered if you want to keep all the smells in the pot. Actually you might have less odor in your kitchen if you leave the lid off; the volatile acids, which otherwise speed up hydrogen sulfide production, can get out of the pot this way.

POTATOES

Finally we come to the third of this triumvirate of proletarian delights, the potato. The potato has fallen on evil times. In the seventeenth century (like many other newly discovered foods) it was widely regarded as an aphrodisiac, too devoted a consumption of which might even shorten a man's life. Devotees became fanatics. In 1664 John Forster spread the Gospel of the Potato in a tract entitled *England's Happiness Increased, or a Sure and Easy Remedy Against all Succeeding Dear Years by a Plantation of the Roots Called Potatoes*.

Once a tasty delicacy, it has been bred into bland conformity to satisfy cravings which must spring from the darkest recesses of the human appetite: french fries and potato chips. Enormous demand and high profits have led to an emphasis on production of varieties that are generally tasteless but make uniform, light-colored fries and chips.

Potatoes fall between two extremes—mealy and waxy. The mealy type is best for french fries and chips, as well as baked and mashed. As if this were not enough to give it the economic upper hand, they are preferred for the preparation of dehydrated potato products. Waxy potatoes are best where firmness, natural flavor, and sweetness are important: boiled potatoes, parsleyed potatoes, potato salad, scalloped potatoes.

The two types are quite different. Mealy potatoes are higher in starch, lower in sugar, swell more in cooking (the starch absorbs a lot of water), tend to have pieces slough off after cooking, and do not brown quickly at high temperatures (not enough sugar in the tuber).

Unfortunately it is not simply a question of going to the grocery store armed with a list of the properties of various potato varieties, and then demanding a Russet Rural or a Russet Burbank. It is simply not known why one potato will cook up mealy and another waxy. Soil, climate, fertilizer—all have their effects. But if you are a true potato fancier, you can separate the two kinds with a simple home "density machine." This is no science-fiction gizmo with sparking electrodes, just a solution of one pound of salt in one gallon of water. Mealy potatoes are denser than waxy ones and will sink in this solution, while the waxy kind float. Some potatoes will be neither one nor the other, and can be fed to uncritical eaters.

AUTODEMONSTRATION H

2 pounds salt
2½ –3 gallons water
assorted potatoes

Dissolve most of the salt in the water. Use a glass container if possible for best visibility. Add the potatoes. If they all sink to the bottom, the solution is not concentrated enough; add more salt until some potatoes rise in the "machine." If they all float, the solution is too concentrated; add more water until some start to sink.

Separate the potatoes, mark them so as to be able to distinguish them, bake, and assay the differences.

Sometimes recipes specify new potatoes. But even with the smallest, roundest, and newest potatoes these recipes may not work. They depend on the potatoes holding their shape after being cooked and browning easily, both characteristics of the waxy variety.

22. NEW POTATOES

- □ 3 pounds small new potatoes (*waxy* variety)
- 12 strips bacon
- 2 teaspoons salt
- 1 teaspoon pepper
- 1 teaspoon vinegar
- 1 teaspoon sugar

Cook the potatoes in boiling water until they are just tender. Drain them, peel them, and dry them with paper towels. Cut into ½-1 inch pieces.

Sauté the bacon until it is well done, remove the meat, and discard half the fat. Sauté the potatoes in the bacon fat until they are brown. Pour off almost all the fat. Crumble the bacon, return it to the sauté pan, add the other ingredients, and cook until they are well mixed. Serve immediately.

23. POTATO SALAD

- □ 2½ pounds small new potatoes (*waxy* variety)
- 1 can (7 ounces/198 milliliters) kernel corn, drained
- 2 green peppers, diced
- 1 teaspoon salt
- ½ teaspoon pepper
- 1½ teaspoons garlic powder
- 1 cup sour cream
- 3 green onions, sliced

Cook the potatoes in boiling water until they are just tender. Drain them, peel them, and chill them. Cut them into 1-inch pieces.

Combine the other ingredients and add the potatoes.

Aside from overcooking, the only problem faced when boiling potatoes is occasional darkening at the stem end. This is caused by the oxidation of an iron-containing compound to form a black product. Prevention is simple. Add some citrus juice or cream of tartar to the cooking water. The citric acid or tartrate interacts strongly with the iron, preventing the formation of the oxidizable compound in the first place.

STORAGE

Potatoes are naturally untrustworthy. They continually change their composition while we look the other way. An interconversion of starch and sugar is continually in action:

$$\textit{starch} \underset{2}{\overset{1}{\rightleftarrows}} \textit{sugar}$$

Reaction 1, which converts starch into sugar, has the same rate no matter what the temperature, but the reverse reaction, converting sugar into starch, is inhibited and becomes very slow below 45°F. Cold storage, where Reaction 1 is faster than 2, leads to a buildup of sugar, and produces a sweet flavor in potatoes, which many people dislike. These tubers needn't be consigned to the pigs. Two or three weeks of warm storage, 70°F+, should render them palatable again.

For best results, potatoes should be stored at temperatures higher than 50°F and in the dark. If left in the light, they may develop green spots on the surface. These sunlight-induced spots contain a toxin, *solanine*. If they appear, cut them out — and cut deeply. If there is still some bitter taste to the tuber, toss it out.

The potato is a member of the nightshade family, as are a number of other tasty foods (tomato, pepper, eggplant), plus some poisonous plants (tobacco and deadly nightshade). Deadly nightshade earns its sinister name by containing the toxins atropine and belladonna.

Another family member, the less well-known black nightshade, also produces solanine, but this chemical disappears as the berries of the plant ripen, and such berries are often used as food.

Sweet potatoes are different. Their tropical origins dictate storage between 55 and 60°F in high humidity, 85 – 90 percent. A tightly sealed plastic bag, moistened inside, will do. But even under these optimum conditions, sweet potatoes do not keep well.

BAKING

The gastronomic problem in baking potatoes is getting the moisture content as you like it. If they come out soggy, some precooking treatments may help. Pricking them with a fork will allow steam to escape during baking. Packing them in rock salt (any salt will do) will draw out some of the moisture. Wrapping in foil gives soft skins, the kind you love to touch. Without the foil the skin dries by evaporation, and an old-fashioned crunchy skin results. Cooking without foil will take slightly less time and will also lead to a less soggy interior. Foil-wrapped items take longer to cook because the metal reflects away some of the heat energy. (We will meet this again when we see how to switch utensils in Chapter 9.)

DEEP-FRYING

Please make sure you have read the section on deep-frying in the preceding chapter so you can defend yourself against an oil fire!

Calamities aside, a difficulty with this technique is gauging the temperature. We are supposed to believe that master chefs rip up pieces of bread, not to feed the local birds, but as offerings thrown into the deep-fry pot to be watched carefully as an augury for a propitious temperature for frying. There are different ways of telling the temperature, depending on which witch doctor you follow:

A 1-inch cube browns in sixty seconds
He is saved who 360 reckons.

I will not trouble you with more wretched verses about bread-browning times, for different kinds of bread will brown at different speeds. Place your confidence solely in a deep-frying thermometer and forget the incantations.

However, bread browning *is* instructive, because it reflects the mechanism for the browning of most deep-fried foods. It is not the hot oil that gives the golden or brown (or black) color to the food at all. Hot oil merely serves as a neutral medium for the transfer of a lot of heat. It is the high-temperature reactions *within the food itself* that give rise to the color changes.

Browning results from what is called the *sugar-amine* reaction. Amines ("ah-means") are parts of protein molecules and will react with sugars when the temperature is high enough. Amines are led through a series of reactions, finally terminating in a sequence so complex it has not yet been pinned down. (It isn't for lack of trying; the mystery of this sequence of reactions plagues the food industry to death.) What is important for us kitchen types is that it is necessary for *both* the sugar *and* the protein to be present for this reaction to be possible. And the more sugar and protein available, the more easily the browning will occur. This is the reason waxy potatoes, high in sugar, brown too quickly to make satisfactory french fries.

We have seen how some very commonplace—even proletarian—foods employ rather exotic and sophisticated chemistry during the cooking process. There is nothing so common to cook that it won't entertain and expand us to think about it.

And remember to watch out for those stuffings.

CHAPTER 3: RÉSUMÉ

I. GARLIC (and onions, leeks, shallots, and chives):

For more flavor:

DO:	Use raw or undercooked items
	Mince finely, mash, or juice

For less flavor:

DO:	Use well-cooked items
	Use whole (or coarsely cut-up) bulbs

II. CABBAGE FAMILY

DO:	Undercook
DON'T:	Overcook
	Use a lid

III. POTATO (white)

	Mealy	*Waxy*
Properties:	Swells when cooked; low sugar, high starch content	Holds shape when cooked; higher sugar content
Storage:	In the dark at temperatures above 50°F	
Sorting:	Denser ("sinkers")	Less dense ("floaters")
Uses:	Baked potato Mashed potato French fries	Boiled potatoes Potato salad Scalloped potatoes Parsleyed potatoes

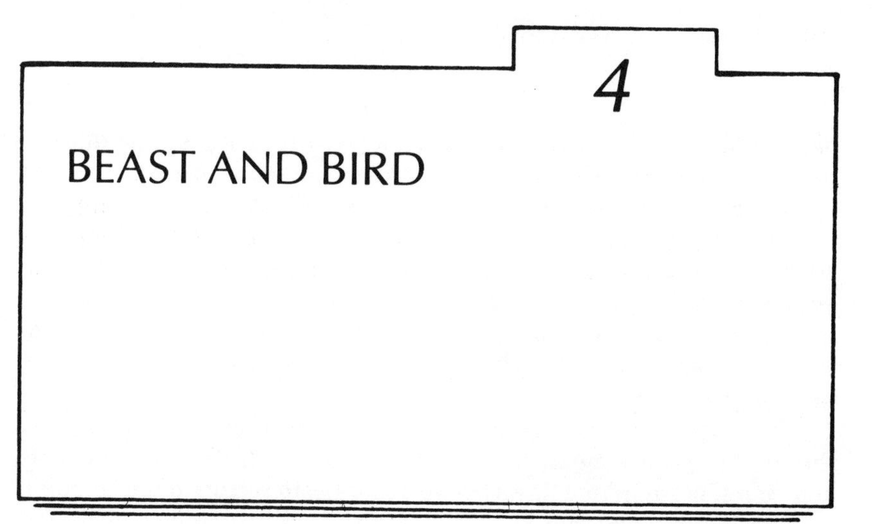

Man has been chewing on meat for a long time — and pondering new ideas to make it tender and tasty. But man's intellect has a formidable enemy, which ultimately will take those protein morsels off his plate — his urge to procreate. As the number of people increases and the traditionally deprived classes and countries become able to buy sufficient protein, each one of us will be eating less of what we desire and more of whatever we can get. So let's talk about how to make it palatable.

TENDERNESS

At least 2,000 years ago the Chinese used marination. Marinades were useful when meats had to stand around without the benefit of refrigeration, because their acid composition retarded bacterial growth. Today cooks often marinate in hopes of tenderizing meat, but the value of modern marinade is chiefly for improving taste.

It is true that the acid component, common to all marinades, will denature meat proteins the same way vinegar helps denature poached egg. But the marinade can only get at the meat proteins on the surface of the meat, and hence the tenderizing effect is only skin deep. Barbecue experts usually grill thick steaks or chops, so most of the meat (everything in the interior) remains unmarinated and tough.

Tenderizers are more effective denaturers than acid marinades. These are natural enzymes, which pull the proteins apart with speed and efficiency. The commonest is an enzyme extracted from the papaya plant and is called *papain* ("pa-pa-yin"). At the time of their conquest by Cortes, the Mexican Indians were tenderizing their meat by wrapping it overnight in bruised papaya leaves.

Tenderizer is probably overqualified for the job at hand. It is so efficient that too long or too liberal an application will result in an overtenderized, mushy texture. And since the enzyme has its maximum activity at 140 – 160°F, holding tenderized meat at warm temperatures, especially when cooked rare, can produce a mushy, unpalatable texture.

Besides papain from papaya, there are two other natural enzymes that will tenderize meat: *bromelin* ("broam-meh-lin") from pineapple and *ficin* ("fissin") from figs. Oriental and Latin recipes often combine fruit with meat, and they should be scrutinized for potential tenderizers. In other words, if your recipe calls for fresh papaya, pineapple and/or figs, do *not* pre-tenderize.

AUTODEMONSTRATION I

3 1-inch cubes of stewing beef
1 cup *fresh* pineapple, pureed

Cut the beef into thin slices. Put the slices from one cube into ½ cup of pineapple puree and do the same for the second set of slices. Let the third set of slices rest by itself in a cup.

Store one of the beef-pineapple cups in the refrigerator, the other, and the beef alone, at room temperature.

After a day, drain and rinse all the samples. Mash a portion of each with a fork, comparing the textures.

The fresh pineapple will tenderize the meat if you have a tough cut. If you fear too mushy a texture but love pineapple with your meat, the solution is simple: use canned rather than fresh pineapple. The high temperature of the canning process destroys the enzyme, and no tenderizing is possible. But with fresh pineapple, papaya, or figs you can play texture games to your pocketbook's content. By increasing the amount of fruit or fresh juice, marination time, and cooking time, and by making the meat chunks smaller, you can tenderize as much as you want.

Conversely, do not expect other fruits to do the work of these special, enzyme-rich ones. Stewing beef, combined with papaya or fresh pineapple, will become naturally tenderized during the cooking process. But such tenderizing action is not the property of peaches or apples or other fruits. If you wish to use non-enzyme-rich fruits, buy a tenderer grade of beef.

Here is a recipe that incorporates natural tenderizers, for those cheaper cuts of meat.

24. TENDERER BEEF

- 2½ cups beef stock or bouillon
- 2½ pounds stewing beef, cut in 1-inch cubes
- ½ teaspoon oregano
- 1 bay leaf
- 1 cup chili sauce
- 1 small can (5½ fluid ounces/156 milliliters) tomato paste
- ½ cup chopped onion
- 1 clove garlic, chopped
- 1 teaspoon cumin powder
- 1 teaspoon salt
- □ 1 cup *fresh* pineapple, crushed
- □ 1 *fresh* papaya, peeled and diced

Puree the chili sauce, tomato paste, onion, garlic, cumin, and salt in a blender until smooth. Add it to the stock with the bay leaf and oregano, boil for 15 minutes, and let cool.

Put a layer of the meat in a casserole. Mix the pineapple and papaya and layer some of it over the meat. Pour a portion of the sauce over these layers. Repeat the layering process until complete.

Refrigerate at least 8 hours.

Preheat the oven to 350°F. Bake for 2 to 3 hours, or until the meat is tender.

Another tenderizing technique, favored by suppliers of high-quality beef to hotels and restaurants, is aging. The meat is kept in special rooms at low temperature (just above the freezing point of water) and constant humidity with ultraviolet light to cut down on bacterial growth, for anywhere from a few days to a few weeks.

It is a lot more effective than artificial methods because the process goes on through the entire section of meat. It is not an elegant process. The animal is on the second half of the ashes-to-ashes, dust-to-dust trip. But the decomposition occurs uniformly throughout the muscle, and the accompanying improvement in taste and tenderness is uniformly produced as well. Unfortunately, such professional techniques are unavailable to most home cooks. *Chacun à son goût*.

DONENESS AND COLOR

Another meaty preoccupation has been the desire to cook-to-a-turn. Before thermometers were available, the experienced cook could test the doneness of the meat by knife, mouth, or color, but best by its resiliency to a prodding finger. Nowadays, although a thermometer is always more accurate, most cooks still pride themselves on their mystical color intuition, so we should know why meat changes color at all.

Practically all meat color changes are due to a pigment called myoglobin ("my-oh-glow-bin"), which receives oxygen from hemoglobin (which has transported it through the bloodstream) and delivers it to the muscle tissue.

Freshly cut beef is purplish-red, but with exposure to air the surface becomes bright cherry red as the myoglobin combines with oxygen and becomes oxymyoglobin:

myoglobin (purplish-red) — *oxygen in air* — *oxymyoglobin (bright red)*

When meat is heated, the interior myoglobin becomes oxygenated to oxymyoglobin, too, and this is what gives rare roast beef its bright red inner color. As the heating continues, the myoglobin protein pigment breaks up and forms the gray-brown compound that we characterize as well-done meat.

Some special situations can lead to unusual colors in meat. Bacterial contamination sometimes produces sulfur compounds, which combine with myoglobin to form greenish compounds. A badly adjusted gas burner or an electric element run at high temperature can also give psychedelic meat — not only will they give off sulfur compounds but carbon monoxide and gaseous nitric oxide as well. The latter two give meat a bright pink color or the red color of cured meat. Sometimes a red color is seen near the surface of a well-cooked fowl. It is then time to see the range repairman, not the butcher.

Veal, pork, lamb, and poultry are not as intensely pigmented as beef, so their color changes are less spectacular and therefore less useful as cooking indicators. For a large piece of meat a roasting thermometer is invaluable. Without it, the cook must depend on the directions in a cookbook, which specify so many minutes of cooking per pound of roast. But this rule-of-thumb roasting does not take into account the age and condition of the meat and of the oven, and they are only useful as a vague approximation.

Roasting meat today has its problems, but it has been made considerably easier than it used to be, as this 1858 description will show.

> Roasting being the most general in use, we will first describe it, although it is not that which was first in practice in cooking, it being evidently an improvement on broiling: we can easily understand how, in the primitive times, when man, finding that his food got covered with the ashes from the fire with which he cooked his meat, would invent a species of grate upon which he could raise the fire, and so cook his meat before it; this early mode of cooking has continued, in many countries, up to the present day, and even in London to within a few years, for I remember seeing in the old Goldsmith's Hall, a fireplace, consisting of stages, on which was laid the wood, and when the meat, and etc. was spitted and arranged before it, the wood was lighted, and a man turned the spits. (It was, no doubt, from arranging the wood thus in stages, that the name of the range was derived.) In many noblemen's castles and ecclesiastical establishments, dogs were kept to turn the spit, from whence we have those of the name of turnspit; whilst in others, where there happened to be a person of a mechanical turn of mind, they applied a water-wheel to the purpose, and the water from it formed a stream in the kitchen, which served as a reservoir for live fish. Different opinions exist as to the mode and the time required for roasting, but this must all depend upon the nature of the fire and the meat. In the Receipts will be found the time which each requires. My plan is to make up as large a fire as the nature of the grate will allow, because I can place my joint near or not, as may be required, and thus obtain every degree of heat.
>
> A new plan of *Roasting by Gas* has latterly come into use, and from the cheapness and cleanliness of the process is likely to become a great favorite.*

*Alexis Soyer, *The Modern Housewife or Ménagère* (London: Simpkin, Marshall and Co., 1858), p. 68.

BROWNING AND ROASTING

An attractive roast does not have to be a matter of luck. A tasty brown crust is within everyone's competence and can be achieved at will by using a process called the Maillard browning reaction — no doubt after a researcher who pursued his gastronomy with scientific devotion. It starts by combining an amino acid (from the meat protein, in this case) and a sugar. This is the complicated reaction that browns french fries. For meat cooked at roasting temperatures it produces an aromatic and tasty crust. We can promote it by *supplying the meat with sufficient sugar at the surface*. Marinades all have some ingredient designed to do this. Here are a few examples.

25. PEANUT BUTTER BARBECUE SAUCE
(2 cups)

- ½ cup peanut butter
- □ ½ cup soy sauce
- ½ cup water
- □ ¼ cup dry sherry
- □ ¼ cup lemon juice
- □ 2 tablespoons honey

Combine all the ingredients in a saucepan and heat gently with stirring until the sauce is smooth.

26. ORANGE BARBECUE SAUCE
(2 cups)

- □ 1 large can (12½ ounces/355 milliliters) frozen orange juice, thawed
- □ ⅓ cup brown sugar
- □ 2 tablespoons lemon juice
- □ 2 tablespoons ketchup
- 3 green onions, thinly sliced
- ½ teaspoon garlic powder
- ½ teaspoon pepper

Mix all the ingredients in a bowl. Use for poultry, ham, or pork.

27. SOY BARBECUE SAUCE

(1½ cups)

- □ 1 cup soy sauce
- □ ¼ cup wine vinegar
- 3 tablespoons dry mustard
- 1 teaspoon garlic powder
- 1 teaspoon salt
- ½ teaspoon pepper
- 4 scallions, chopped
- 4 tablespoons chives, chopped
- □ 4 tablespoons brown sugar

Heat all the ingredients in a saucepan until the sugar is dissolved.

The crucial ingredients in these marinades are the acids (vinegar, citrus juice) for a bit of tenderizing and the sugars (ketchup, sugar, soy sauce) for browning. Here is an application:

28. BARBECUED RIBS

- 6 pounds beef ribs
- □ 1½ cups Soy Barbecue Sauce (Recipe 27)

Marinate the ribs for 2 or 3 hours in the sauce, turning occasionally.

Barbecue over a hot fire, *basting frequently with the sauce* until the meat is well done and crusty.

The soy sauce and brown sugar provide enough sugars for the browning reaction. Almost any sugar can combine with the meat proteins to produce a deep color and luscious flavor compounds, with one grave exception—sucrose, table sugar. But this sugar can be transformed into reactive sugars by heating in the presence of acid. It is comforting that all the barbecue sauces that contain sugar also have vinegar or lemon juice to supply the acid for this reaction.

Here is an example using lamb:

29. INDONESIAN GRILLED LAMB

- 3 pounds leg of lamb, cut in 1-inch cubes (pork can substitute)
- □ 2 cups Peanut Butter Barbecue Sauce (Recipe 25)

Marinate the meat in the sauce for 2 to 3 hours in the refrigerator. Thread the meat on skewers and grill over a hot fire, basting frequently with the sauce, until the meat is well browned and done to your taste.

In the next sauce the sugar is in the ketchup, and the acid is supplied by lime juice.

30. BARBECUED CHICKEN

- 6 chicken legs and thighs (about 3 pounds)
- □ 1⅓ cup ketchup
- □ ⅔ cup *unsweetened* lime juice
- 1 clove garlic, chopped
- 1 teaspoon salt
- 1 teaspoon dry mustard

Heat all the ingredients, except the chicken, in a saucepan until the mixture is well blended. Remove from the heat.

Marinate the chicken in the sauce for 2 to 3 hours in the refrigerator.

Preheat the oven to 400°F. Lay the chickens in one or more greased ovenproof casseroles. Bake for 1 hour, turning and basting occasionally.

Once more the ingenuity of our gastronomic heritage has connected science with art.

Some meats (beef, liver, cured meats) have a large enough sugar content to brown easily, but we can regulate the color, thickness, and hardness by adjusting the roasting temperature and especially the steam environment.

Whenever roasting is done in an oven, the meat is in a moist atmosphere. The evaporating juices have no escape hatch, so humidity builds up within the oven. Opening the oven lessens it, but roasting with a cover on or with stock at the bottom of the roaster intensifies it and gives a lighter, thinner, and softer crust. Basting with a water-based sauce will also create steam and reduce the browning.

This is why it is so difficult to recreate a barbecue dish successfully in the oven. Barbecuing is a true dry-heat method and gives a darker, thicker, and crisper crust. These differences are reinforced by the temperature as well. High temperature rapidly evaporates the meat's juices from the outer layer, thickening and crisping it; moreover the browning reactions, like most reactions, are accelerated at high temperatures.

Wrapping in foil will reduce crust formation in two ways. Foil is a good heat insulator — a radiant heat shield like the makeshift one deployed by the first Skylab astronauts to keep the spacecraft from cooking to death. A foil-wrapped roast cooks at a lower temperature, for a longer time, and has less crust than would an unwrapped bird sitting beside it in the oven. Moreover the foil envelope around the roast also holds in the moisture, thus stewing rather than roasting it. The result is not only much less crust, but, as tests have shown, meat that is less tender, less juicy, and less flavorful. Anyone who uses foil when "roasting" shouldn't.

In today's energy purgatory, there is a simple way to cook meat more quickly and yet use *less* fuel — with skewers. Skewers pipe heat into the interior of the roast with extraordinary efficiency. Cooking time can be reduced a third or more, and there will also be less weight loss. But the meat will be less tender than otherwise. The decision is then whether to use the energy of the oven or of your jaw.

Enough research has already gone into the prospect of mastication to determine that 325°F is the best compromise temperature for roasting tender cuts. This is a slow and long cooking process and has consequences for dishes like Yorkshire pudding which are cooked simultaneously with the beef.

Soyer's version, below, worked well because the high temperature helped vaporize moisture and thereby leaven the pudding. And since it cooked directly underneath the beef, lots of drippings fell on it automatically.

Yorkshire Pudding

Put six tablespoonfuls of flour into a basin, with six eggs, a pinch of salt, and a quarter of a pint of milk, mix well together with a wooden spoon, adding the remaining three-quarters of a pint of milk by degrees; you have previously set a shallow tin dish *under a piece of roasting beef* [my italics] before the fire; an hour before serving pour in the batter, leaving it under the meat until quite set and rather browned upon the top, then turn the pudding over upon the dish you intend serving it upon, and again place it before the fire until the other side is rather browned, when it is ready to serve with the meat.

This pudding is very excellent *baked under a small piece of beef* of about five or six pounds. It is also frequently baked beneath a shoulder of mutton; and sometimes in an oven separate, if the fire is not large enough (with a few spoonfuls of gravy added).*

Since lower roasting temperatures will not give enough "spring" for the leavening, a modern recipe for Yorkshire pudding cooks it separately from the roast. Notice how hot the oven must be in this version.

31. YORKSHIRE PUDDING

1 cup flour
1 teaspoon salt
1 cup milk
3 eggs
¼ cup (approx.) bacon fat or pan drippings

Preheat the oven to 450°F.

Pour the fat onto two 6-cup muffin tins so as to coat the cups completely. Place them in the oven until the fat *just starts to smoke.*

Combine all the other ingredients in the container of an electric blender and blend at high speed for 30 seconds.

When the fat is ready, pour the batter into the muffin cups. Fill each cup about ¾ full. Bake for 10 minutes, then turn the puddings upside down in their cups and bake 10 minutes more, or until they are brown and crisp on top.

You really don't need two ovens to enjoy this dish with roast beef. The roast benefits by "resting" out of the oven long enough for you to whip up some Yorkshire Pudding.

*Ibid., p. 272.

STUFFING (again)

The sheer bulk of a Thanksgiving turkey may lead a nervous cook to crank up the oven temperature. After all, instead of waiting 5½ to 6 hours for a 22-pound bird to cook at 300 to 330°F, why not roast it at 450°F for only about 3½ hours? Here the cooking may be too quick; the outer part of the turkey will be overdone before the interior gets hot enough. And "hot enough" does not mean warm enough to swallow; it means hot enough to keep you out of the hospital.

As we mentioned in the last chapter, in stuffings even onions, if unsautéed, may not get cooked well enough for palatability. Most stuffings are susceptible to bacterial contamination, but some are more dangerous than others. Sausage, giblet, egg, oyster, and cornbread types typically have high bacterial counts, whereas the fruit-based stuffings are lesser risks because their acidity keeps down the bug population.

32. GIBLET LIVER STUFFING

(8 cups)

2 cups chicken giblets
½ pound calf's liver, cut up
4 tablespoons butter
2 onions, chopped
2 cloves garlic, chopped
½ teaspoon sweet (Spanish) paprika
½ cup red or white wine
6 cups fresh bread, cubed
1 teaspoon sesame oil
1 teaspoon dill
1 teaspoon salt
½ teaspoon pepper
1 egg

Cook the giblets (except the livers) in boiling water until tender, about 1 hour. Drain well.

Sauté the calf's liver, all the giblets, the onions, garlic and paprika in butter until the meat is tender. Remove the mixture from the pan and chop it very fine, then mix in the other ingredients.

33. FRUIT STUFFING

(4 cups)

- □ ¾ cups fresh cranberries, picked over
- ⅓ cup water
- 6 tablespoons sugar
- 2 tablespoons brown sugar
- □ 1¼ cups crushed pineapple, well drained
- □ ½ cup golden seedless raisins
- □ 4 tablespoons lemon juice
- 1 teaspoon salt
- ⅛ teaspoon pepper
- 4 cups stale or toasted bread, cubed

Place the berries, water and both sugars in a small saucepan and boil, stirring occasionally, until the berries burst (about 5 minutes).

Combine all the ingredients except the bread and mix well, then mix in the bread.

[*Note:* 1 can (14 fluid ounces/398 milliliters) of whole berry cranberry sauce can substitute for the fresh cranberries, water and both sugars. Start the recipe with the second paragraph.]

The fruit-based stuffing does not require prior cooking because the acidity from the fruit and lemon juice keeps the bacterial counts low.

SOUPS, STEWS, AND SAUTÉS

At the other end of the temperature (and elegance) scale of meat cookery is soup-making. It is of course the most nutritious way of eating meat, since we consume the cooking water. The connective tissue in meat contains a lot of collagen, which long, slow cooking transforms to gelatin. A good soup will "set" in the refrigerator because it has become a gelatin.

Some cookbooks advocate starting a soup by putting the meat in cold, rather than simmering, water. The theory is that an impermeable pellicle (film) is formed by the high temperature, and this hinders the extraction of the good flavors. Experiments done in the 1930's determined that this was not true — the temperature is just not high enough to form a pellicle.

34. BEEF STOCK

(2 quarts)

- 3 pounds stewing beef, preferably with the bone in
- 3 or 4 beef marrowbones
- 3 quarts water
- 4 stalks celery, cut up, leaves included
- 2 onions, sliced
- 1 leek, sliced
- 2 cups stewed tomatoes, drained
- 2 large carrots, sliced
- 3 cloves garlic
- 1 turnip, diced
- 2 sprigs parsley
- 2 bay leaves
- 3 sprigs dill
- 10 peppercorns
- 4 teaspoons salt

Put everything in a large kettle, bring to a boil, reduce the heat and simmer, *covered*, for 3 hours.

Strain the broth and refrigerate overnight. The fat that congeals on the surface may be discarded before the stock is reheated.

Serve the meat as Boiled Beef or use for preparing a dish like hash.

The meat is put in at the start of the cooking, but the water temperature is not critical. What *is* critical is that the meat should not be sautéed or cooked at a temperature high enough to seal it up. This is done when we are cooking a stew, where the flavor is expected to remain largely in the meat.

Thus you can control where the flavor will be localized—in the liquid or in the solid. In the former (soups), no sautéing; in the latter (stews), sauté the meat first, as in the next recipe.

35. BEEF STEW WITH BURGUNDY

- ¼ cup flour
- 1 teaspoon salt
- 1 teaspoon pepper
- 4 tablespoons olive oil
- 3 pounds stewing beef, cut in 1-inch cubes
- 4 green onions, sliced
- 2 cloves garlic, sliced
- 4 onions, sliced
- 1 cup mushrooms, sliced
- 2 carrots, thinly sliced
- 1½ cups Burgundy (or other dry red wine)
- 2 sprigs parsley
- 2 sprigs dill
- 2 bay leaves
- 2 tablespoons ketchup

Mix the salt and pepper into the flour and coat the beef with it.

Heat the olive oil in a sauté pan. *Quickly sauté the floured beef until the cubes are browned all over*. Transfer the meat to a casserole.

Brown the onions and garlic in the first sauté pan (use more oil if necessary) and add them to the casserole. Now add the other ingredients to the casserole.

Cover and cook at the simmer for 3 hours.

In this stew the beef is sautéed, as it invariably is, before it is put to cook in the sauce. The meat is encapsulated in its own sauté jacket, and it retains its characteristic taste instead of letting it leak out.

And when sautéing, remember that quickness and high temperature pay off by helping the browning reaction. Beef contains enough

natural sugar in its tissues so that sautéing in hot fat develops a nice brown coating from the sugar-amine reaction. But if the temperature drops, the meat cooks to the gray color of stewed meat. Meat must be the *first* item in the hot fat, so that it cooks at a high temperature. If unbreaded vegetables were done first, the energy expended vaporizing some of their moisture would lower the fat temperature too much, and the browning would be drastically hindered.

Do not make the mistake of sautéing too many pieces of meat at once. The room-temperature meat cools off the fat just as surely as ice cubes chill tap water. So use steely self-control, brown just a few pieces at a time to keep the fat hot, and think how much better it will be than hamburger or hot dog.

CURED MEAT

Of the two American favorites designed to turn an aesthete's stomach, the hamburger must yield foremost place to the hot dog. Food poisoning engendered by overdoing the dogs is rare, however. The manufacturers add a liberal quantity of nitrite (or nitrate) to the sausage mixture, which knocks off the microbes that might cause us trouble. Nitrite also develops a bright red color in the meat, which is widely regarded as a sales come-on.

But, as so often happens, the solution to one problem leads to new and more serious ones. For the nitrite reacts with the meat proteins, pulls off some of the amino acids and forms compounds called *nitrosamines* ("nye-trow-sa-means"), which are extraordinarily effective carcinogens. They cause cancer at the drop of a hat. They are not present in very high concentrations in the wiener, but there is a growing fear — not yet verging on certain knowledge — that the nitrites will react with amino acids *in our stomachs* to produce these nitrosamines.

But would I present you with all this doomsday talk if I were not able to provide a solution? Of course not! And the solution is to boycott commercial sausages and learn the pleasures of making sausage yourself — at home and free of nitrite. A good butcher will have, or can obtain for you, sausage casing, which can fit onto an attachment for your meat grinder, and that is all you need. (If you cannot find these items, just shape the meat into patties.)

Try the two recipes on the following page for starters:

36. MOTHER'S NATURAL HOME-MADE SAUSAGE WITH SPANISH SEASONING
(for 2 pounds sausage)

2 pounds ground pork or other meat
2 teaspoons salt
1 teaspoon paprika (Spanish)
1 teaspoon black pepper
¼ teaspoon cayenne pepper
(garlic, onion optional)

37. MOTHER'S NATURAL HOME-MADE SAUSAGE WITH NORTH AMERICAN SEASONING
(for 2 pounds sausage)

2 pounds ground pork or other meat
2 teaspoons salt
2 teaspoons ground sage
1 teaspoon ground black pepper
¼ teaspoon garlic powder
¼ teaspoon onion powder
¼ teaspoon chili powder

Mix 2 pounds ground pork with one of the seasoning mixes.

Slip the sausage casing on the grinder attachment and wash well, inside and out, under cold water. Start off with short sections until you get the feel of it. Assemble the grinder without the cutter and force the meat into the casing. Do not overfill. Tie off the far end with string and twist the casing to form links. Tie off the end near the grinder.

Use immediately or store in the freezer.

To pan-fry, start in a cold skillet and fry over moderate heat until well browned and completely done — 10 to 15 minutes.

If sausages scorch, try this technique: Cook in ⅛ inch of water in a skillet with a tight-fitting lid. After 10 minutes of this steaming, pour off the liquid and brown the sausages by frying them for 5 to 10 minutes or more with the lid off.

If this de-emphasis on commercial sausage seems eccentric, let me tell you about a talk given at a Meat Industry Research Conference.

The paper was entitled "Nutritional Aspects of Offal Proteins" and reported on the amino-acid composition of bladder, lips, snout, intestine, udder, windpipe, and cheek — among other delightful items — of cattle and pigs. All had been studied "with a view to their utilization as an economical protein material for human consumption."

Perhaps the thing to do to live through protein scarcity and the indifference of the economic establishment is to develop our tastes in unusual but nevertheless traditional directions. Brains, easy to digest and prepare, are very nutritious and delicious. And what about horse, tasty and toothsome?

CHAPTER 4: RÉSUMÉ

I. TENDERIZING

A. Marinades

DO:	Include an acid
	Include a sugar
DON'T:	Expect more than a superficial effect

B. Natural and Artificial

DO:	Use raw pineapple, fig, or papaya, or commercial tenderizer
DON'T:	Overtenderize
	Expect more than a superficial effect

II. BROWNING AND ROASTING

For a dark, thick crust:

DO:	Use high heat
	Use long cooking times
	Use sugar-containing coatings or marinades
DON'T:	Wrap or cover

For a dark, thin crust:

DO:	Use a short cooking time

For a light, thin crust:

DO:	Use low or moderate heat
	Wrap in foil or cover
	Baste with water-based sauce to generate steam

DON'T: Use a sugar-containing coating or marinade

III. STUFFING

DO: Use fruit-based stuffing without *pre*cooking
Precook other stuffings outside the bird, then stuff and roast immediately
Bake stuffings separately for greatest safety
Refrigerate excess after the meal

IV. SOUPS, STEWS, AND SAUTÉS

DO: Sauté meats until brown when preparing stews
DON'T: Sauté meats when preparing soups

V. CURED MEATS

DO: Prepare your own sausages:
Buy casing from a butcher, rinse it well under running water, stuff using an attachment on a meat grinder, refrigerate (for a few days at most) or freeze
Realize patties are an alternative

5

FISH: FOOD FOR THOUGHT

There are so many ways to be nervous about fish. Hypochondriacs fear choking on fish bones. Nervous students futilely gobble fish as "brain-food." Grocers count down to spoilage. Marriages founder on arguments over how to kill live lobsters. And hostesses dread having to serve dry, overcooked fish.

This is unfortunate, for fish can satisfy every taste, and its preparation should involve no more anxiety than does poaching an egg.

POACHING

Here are four court bouillons, suitable for cooking fish.

38. VINEGAR COURT BOUILLON

(2 quarts)

1½ quarts water
1 onion, sliced
1 carrot, sliced
2 stalks celery (with leaves), cut in 1-inch lengths
1 *branch* parsley
1 *branch* dill
1 teaspoon salt
6 peppercorns
□ 2 cups vinegar

Bring everything, except the vinegar, to a boil in a covered pot for 15 minutes. Add the vinegar, re-cover, and *simmer* for 5 minutes more.

39. WINE COURT BOUILLON

(2 quarts)

Same recipe as above, but substitute □ 2 cups of dry white wine for the vinegar.

40. MILK AND LEMON COURT BOUILLON

(2 quarts)

1½ quarts water
2 cups milk
□ 3 lemons, sliced
□ 3 lemons, juice of

Bring the water, lemons, and lemon juice to a boil in a covered pot for 5 minutes. Add the milk slowly and bring to a *simmer*. (The milk may curdle, but this is just an aesthetic problem, not a functional one.)

41. BEER COURT BOUILLON

(2 quarts)

1 quart water
□ 1 quart beer
1 teaspoon salt
1 teaspoon pepper
3 tablespoons sugar (less if you use dark beer)

Add all the ingredients to a pot, cover, and bring to a *simmer*.

In each of these "broths" there is some ingredient that is acidic—vinegar, dry wine, lemon, or beer—and any good court bouillon *must* contain something acidic. Acids help us get rid of the unpleasant fishy odors and allow us to appreciate the subtle flavors that would otherwise be masked. Thus, it is not merely a question of personal or national preference that these recipes all contain an acidic element.

Fishy odors are caused by some remarkably simple molecules, all of which are called amines because they are formed with a nitrogen-containing group of atoms, the amino group.

$$R-NH_2$$

another group of atoms   *amino group*

Fishy odors are analogues of this class of molecules; they are very small, so they have a high volatility, one of the reasons they are so potent, nose-wise. And they *are* potent since they comprise only 0.0001 percent of the fish's weight! But their simple chemistry has, for centuries, allowed cooks to eliminate them very easily.

The nitrogen in the amino group will pick up any protons (H^+) in the area to form the charged $NH_3{}^+$ species:

$$\underset{\textit{uncharged}}{R-NH_2 + H^+} \qquad \underset{\textit{charged}}{R-NH_3{}^+}$$

All that is needed is a high-enough density of protons around, so that the reaction has a chance. Since an acid is, by definition, a solution with an excess of protons, when a fish is put into acidic court bouillon, all of the fishy amines react to change themselves from uncharged molecules to charged ones.

The importance of this process is that the amine changes its electrical character. Uncharged organic molecules are generally hard to dissolve in water ("Oil and water don't mix"). But charged ones will dissolve very easily and will be tightly bound to the water, and once they are stuck there we have immobilized the odors; they cannot get to our noses.

Normally the serving of lemon-garnished fingerbowls after a meal is an affectation. With a dinner at which the entrée is meat, in fact, a packet of detergent would be more useful than the lemon, because the diner principally needs to remove grease. But with a fish dinner—particularly a lobster dinner, since lobster is handled with the fingers more than, say, trout—such a service is highly useful. The citric acid from the lemon helps dissolve the fishy amines off the diner's fingers and puts them into solution in the fingerbowl water.

AUTODEMONSTRATION J

2 pieces fish fillet, 1-inch square, at room temperature
2 bowls of water, ½ cup each
2 tablespoons lemon juice

Put the lemon juice into *one* of the bowls of water and stir.
Add a piece of fish to each bowl. Wait 5 minutes.
Remove the fish, rinse them, and smell each one.

Now that you are convinced that any proper court bouillon must be acidic, you can devise your own recipe, substituting grapefruit juice, for example, as the active ingredient.

42. POACHED WHOLE FISH

1 whole salmon (or trout, halibut, red snapper, cod, or striped bass), gutted
2 quarts court bouillon (use a volume consonant with the size of the cooking vessel; the fish should be covered by the liquid)

Truss the fish with string or wrap in cheesecloth and tie up. If you have a fish poacher, *lay the fish on the rack*, put it in the poacher, add the liquid until the fish is covered. Cover the poacher and bring the liquid to the *simmering point*.

Cooking time can be judged two reliable ways: *either* insert a thermometer into the thickest part of the flesh and cook until the temperature reaches 140°F (60°C), *or* test with a skewer by inserting it into the same region; the fish is cooked when it goes in easily.

To serve, remove the skin and fins.

Fish is *very* tender after it is cooked; it will need help to hold itself together. Lace it or wrap it. A support is a good idea also, especially one that will keep it out of contact with a possibly superheated bottom pot surface.

When a fish is done, the flesh looks milky and opaque, rather than watery and translucent, and flakes easily.

Fish should never be boiled; large bubbles and general turbulence will break up the tender flesh. Simmering gets the job done in a much gentler fashion.

A large thick fish should be started in cold court bouillon so the temperature increase will be gradual and the cooking more even. If you start a big fish in hot court bouillon, the outer part will be overcooked before the inside is done.

Starting the cooking in hot liquid is suitable for thinner items like halibut steak, which *no one* is going to spend time lacing or wrapping. The high temperature quickly firms up the outer layer just enough to help hold it in one piece.

Another poached fish delicacy is the fish dumpling. In the high echelons of gastronomy it is called a *quenelle*, includes whipped cream and/or eggs, and is very airy. Here is a more down-to-earth version with egg serving as a binding agent to hold the balls together.

43. RUTH'S GEFILTE FISH

- 3 pounds whitefish and/or yellow pike, filleted
- fish bones
- 2 onions, quartered
- 3 onions, sliced
- 3 eggs
- ⅓ cup water
- ¼ cup matzo meal (or crushed soda crackers)
- 4 carrots, sliced diagonally
- salt and pepper
- □ 1 lemon, sliced

Wash and clean the fish bones. Add them, with the lemon and sliced onion, to a large pot, add enough water to cover and simmer for 30 minutes.

Grind the fish, using a medium disk in the grinder. Pass the fish through again, this time including the quartered onions. Put this mixture in a large bowl and add all the other ingredients except the carrot. Chop (or pound with a pestle) the mixture thoroughly. Shape into ovoids, the size of a large egg.

Add the carrot to the pot; add more water and bring to a *slow simmer*.

Add the fish *gently*, using a ladle. The fish should be covered with water. Cover the pot and cook slowly for 2½ to 3 hours. Replenish the water if necessary.

Remove the pot from the heat, let cool, and remove the fish carefully with a ladle. Garnish each with a carrot slice. They may be served hot or cold, with a strong horseradish.

There is one fish preparation where the acid not only has an effect on the odor, but also cooks the dish. Acid can denature and "cook" fish protein just as certainly as vinegar helps denature the poached egg. Try this next experiment to prove it to yourself.

AUTODEMONSTRATION K

- 3 pieces (1-inch square) of ¼-inch thick fish fillet
- 2 cups water
- 1 cup vinegar

Cut each fish square into 16 pieces, i.e., ¼-inch cubes. Put one group of 16 in a cup of water and the second in the cup of vinegar.

Cook the third set for 5 minutes in one cup of simmering water in a pot. Cool.

Cover all three and put them in the refrigerator for a day. Remove a piece from each of the three sets and, comparing the firmnesses and textures, mash them with a fork.

The acetic acid of the vinegar has denatured the fish proteins, firming the texture and making it edible. Note the difference between the result of slow reaction at low temperature and fast denaturation at the high temperature of simmering water.

Now try this recipe, especially recommended for the energy-conscious, bombed-out, or overheated cook.

44. SEVICHE

2 pounds fish fillet, cut into ½-inch squares
1 red hot pepper
1 green hot pepper
1 yellow pepper
2 tablespoons chopped green onion
1 tomato, diced
½ teaspoon garlic powder
1 teaspoon salt
1 teaspoon sugar
□ 1 cup fresh lime juice (about 4 limes)

Discard the stems, seeds, and internal ribs of the peppers and dice them finely. Combine them with the other ingredients in a *glass or ceramic bowl* and refrigerate overnight or until the fish turns white and opaque. Drain off the excess liquid.

Serve as an appetizer or as the central element of a vegetable salad.

The citric acids of the citrus juices have "cooked" the fish by acidity and without heat!

STEAMING

A really excellent way to cook fish is by steaming; the fish does not dry out and it is automatically supported by the steamer rack, so no lacing or wrapping is required.

45. STEAMED SOLE WITH BLACK BEAN SAUCE
(2 portions)

- 1½ pounds sole fillet
- 2 tablespoons Oriental-style salted black beans
- ½ cup hot water
- 2 green onions
- 2 teaspoons soy sauce
- □ 1 tablespoon sherry
- 1 tablespoon bland oil
- 1 tablespoon minced fresh ginger
- ½ teaspoon salt

Set a wok (a round-bottomed Oriental-style pan) containing a few inches of water on the range and heat to boiling. (See pages 25 – 26 for alternative utensils for steaming.)

Meanwhile soak the black beans in ½ cup hot water for 15 minutes. When they have plumped, mince them, saving only 2 tablespoons of the minced beans. Mince the heads of the scallions and cut up the green parts. Combine the 2 tablespoons of beans, the scallions, soy, sherry, oil, ginger, and salt.

Grease a steamer rack, put the fish on a plate at least one inch narrower than the inside of the rack, and pour the seasonings over it. Cover and steam 20 to 25 minutes or until the fish is firm.

STEAMED FISH

There is absolutely no problem of turbulence here; the fish has been elevated away from the harsh action going on in the boiling water.

But the acidic ingredient is still there to charge up the amines and wash them into the liquid water.

The next technique to consider might be baking if there were not a way of cooking fish that is halfway between steaming and baking. The idea is to encase the entire preparation in a paper or aluminum bag, which seals in the vapors so the fish is "steamed" while the bag "bakes" in the oven. It is called cooking *en papillote*.

EN PAPILLOTTE

46. BAGGED HALIBUT
(2 portions)

- 2 halibut steaks, ¾-inch thick
- □ 2 tablespoons lemon juice
- ¼ cup dry bread crumbs
- ¼ cup Parmesan cheese
- 1 teaspoon basil
- ½ teaspoon oregano
- ½ teaspoon garlic powder
- ⅛ teaspoon pepper
- 12 fresh shrimp, shelled and deveined
- □ 4 tablespoons dry sherry

Preheat the oven to 350°F.

Cut 4 sheets of aluminum foil (heavy gauge) or heavy (parchment) paper into 12-inch squares. Lay out 2 sheets and grease them on one side. Place a fish steak on each and sprinkle them with lemon juice.

Mix the bread crumbs with the cheese, basil, oregano, garlic powder and pepper. Sprinkle *half* this mixture on the steaks. Lay 6 shrimp on each steak and sprinkle on the remaining half of the bread-crumb mixture and the sherry.

Grease one side of the remaining 2 sheets, place them (greased side down) on the preparation, and fold over the edges, crimping them to make a tight seal. Do not roll up the edges too close to the fish, for there should be slack for vapor expansion.

Bake in the oven for 20 to 25 minutes. Open the packets at the table.

Just as in steaming, the fish is held regally aloft, surrounded by a moist atmosphere but not buffeted about by bubbles. There is the problem of getting at the fish to test for doneness, so some experimentation with cooking times is in order. (Of course you can always pull one packet out of the oven and unwrap it a bit to peek in and test the contents.) Also, keep in mind that any sauce you use *in* the bag will be thinned by the moisture released during cooking, so make it extra thick.

If your spouse has taken the fish poacher as part of the divorce settlement, try this technique instead. You can cook a really large fish with no more apparatus than a roll of aluminum foil, and the aroma released when the papillotte is opened at the table will reconcile any suitor to child support.

BAKING AND BROILING

When cooking fish at high temperatures, the trick is to keep it from drying out. You have your choice of two solutions: provide moisture or provide insulation.

Moisture can be supplied by basting the outside or, from within, by using a stuffing designed to give off moisture during cooking. Mushrooms and other high-water-content foods are perfect for this.

Insulating a fish can be accomplished by wrapping it with vine leaves or something else that is flexible and has a high moisture content. Aluminum foil will also insulate the exterior a bit. The tastiest way is to use an edible coating as the insulation.

47. DROWNED SOLE

- 6 sole fillets
- □ 3 tomatoes, sliced
- □ 2 cups thick sour cream
- ¾ cup tomato paste
- 2 tablespoons capers
- 1 teaspoon salt
- ½ teaspoon pepper

Preheat the oven to 350°F.

Grease two casseroles, lay the fish in them and cover them evenly with the tomato slices.

Mix the other ingredients together and *pour them over the fish.* Bake for 30 minutes, or until the fish is done.

BAKED FISH

Another insulating coating can be built up from bread crumbs.

48. CRUMB-COATED TURBOT

- 4 to 6 turbot fillets
- □ 1 cup dry bread crumbs
- □ 2 cups yogurt
- ½ cup dark beer
- 2 tablespoons dill
- 2 tablespoons caraway seeds
- 1 teaspoon salt
- ½ teaspoon pepper

Preheat the oven to 350°F.

Grease one or more ovenproof casseroles and lay the fish in them.

Mix everything else thoroughly, and use this mixture to coat the fish. Bake for 30 minutes or until the fish is done.

FRYING

Probably the most universally malpracticed methods of preparing fish are pan-frying and deep-frying. The entire object of the cook should be to seal the outer skin of the fish as fast as possible, so it will cook without absorbing oil or grease. But if the oil is not hot enough, no crust or coating will form, and the finished product will have performed like a sponge — not the sort of seafood we had in mind.

Even if you do get your oil to the right temperature, success is not guaranteed. If too much fish is put into the oil at one time, its temperature will be reduced so much that the results will be vastly unappetizing. For example, if corn oil is heated to a temperature just below that at which it starts smoking, 400°F, and an equal weight of fish at room temperature, 70°F, is dumped in, the temperature of the fish plus oil system will end up somewhere between 200 and 300°F. Not good!

When pan-frying, if the fish starts to stick to the pan, the oil was not hot enough to form the crust quickly.

Fish is often floured, breaded, or coated with a batter when it is to be fried. There is a good scientific reason for this. The coating soaks up the water of the surface layers of the fish, preventing it from vaporizing. Otherwise, if your fish is damp, the water is converted to steam by the hot fat, and the temperature of the oil is lowered because of all the energy expended in driving off the water; the fish ends up soggy with water and heavy with oil.

Moreover, the temperature at which frying is done is so high there is a good chance the outside of the fish will overcook. A coating serves the same function as it did for baking. And the more extreme the temperature, the thicker the coating. So pan-fried fish are usually just given a dusting of flour while deep-fried fish are batter-coated.

49. BETTER BEER BATTER

(2 cups)

- 2 cups flour
- 14 ounces beer, flat
- 2 eggs
- 1 teaspoon garlic powder
- 1 tablespoon sugar
- 1 teaspoon pepper
- 1 teaspoon onion powder

Mix the ingredients thoroughly, but do not beat too much. If the batter is too thin, add more flour. It should "plop" from a spoon.

BATTERED FISH

So let's fry some fish.

50. BATTERED FISH

3 pounds fish fillets, cut in pieces
□ 2 cups Better Beer Batter (Recipe 49)
cooking oil for deep-frying

Dry each piece of fish thoroughly with paper towels. Heat the cooking oil for deep frying to 375°F (190°C). Coat each piece of fish with the batter and deep-fry for 5 to 10 minutes, turning the pieces occasionally. Drain the fried fish quickly on paper towels and serve at once.

STORAGE

No matter how a fish is cooked, it must first be bought (or caught) and perhaps stored. The frozen-fish and food-chain industries have had many economic effects, but one of the most regrettable has been the demise of the fresh fish market.

In some big cities a few large fish markets remain. When I can, I like to wander through one of these, gazing at tables of reproachful fish bedded in ice. Their reproach cuts no ice with me. I return their stare to determine which has the clearest eyes. A dull white eye (in the fish, of course) indicates that it has been around too long. After death, moisture evaporates from the tissues, and they become opaque.

The spoilage of fish is related to their heroism. As befits wild animals, fish do not go gently into the net. They put up a good struggle. This does not save them but it does set in motion a series of biochemical reactions which, in pre-refrigeration days, used to provide some protection for the species as a whole. These reactions made fish carcasses start stinking up the place very quickly. So you only caught as much as you could consume right away or could bear to eat as dried or salted fish.

The death struggle of the fish promotes its own decomposition, for the following reason: When muscular energy is expended quickly, it is supplied by *glycogen* ("gly-koh-jen"), which is stored in the muscle tissue. Glycogen is an agglomeration of molecules of the simple sugar glucose and, when needed, can be broken down quickly to the easily metabolized glucose. Animals that are well-rested and calm when slaughtered have high levels of glycogen reserve, and after death these begin a series of chemical decompositions resulting in the production of lactic acid (the acid in milk), which acts as a sort of preservative. A fierce struggle, on the other hand, uses up the glycogen, so there is no production of lactic acid to act as a preservative, and flesh spoils quickly.

With the coming of the commercial ice industry in the early nineteenth century, huge catches of fish could be stored up and delivered to shore in first-rate condition, regardless of the creatures' death struggle. But even so, fish will taste best if it is cooked as soon as possible after it is bought.

One example of the difficulty of storing seafood is the usual failure encountered when one tries to keep lobsters alive in a bathtub. A tubful of tap water, even cool and running, will kill off these marine crustaceans in no time. Lobsters and other saltwater organisms are happy in fish-market holding tanks only because these contain salt water. The absence of salt in the lobster's environment is a mortal disaster of the same magnitude as the absence of oxygen would be in ours.

The cellular material of all living things is contained by a membrane that can pass water. But most of the solutes which make up the inner medium of the cell's existence cannot cross this barrier. When a saltwater fish is in its natural habitat, there is no imbalance across this membrane that cannot be handled by a little work on the part of the cell. But if this fish is put in fresh water, then there is an imbalance of salt concentrations across this membrane, and a natural force, called osmosis, is set in motion. Its blind object is to equalize the concentrations. The only mechanism available is the transport of water through this membrance, since it is impermeable to almost everything else. So water is forced through the membrane into the cell, diluting its salt content.

salt water

membrane — — — — — — — — — — — —

cell liquid
(salty)

(a) Saltwater fish in salt water

fresh water

H_2O H_2O H_2O

membrane — — — — — — — — — *OSMOSIS*

cell liquid

(diluted, less salty)

(b) Saltwater fish in fresh water

The consequence of this rapid influx of water is that the cell becomes so diluted that it cannot function and ultimately so distended that it bursts. Just one such misstep can do in your favorite crustacean.

The prospect of impending world protein shortages makes it more likely that we will be eating more fish and less beef in the future. This may well turn out to be a blessing for gastronomy, nutrition, and even our characters. If the daily news reports are depressing, eat a fish, remember how heroic they are, and resolve to face the next day with as much confidence as a salmon.

CHAPTER 5: RÉSUMÉ

I. POACHING

DO: Use an acidic court bouillon
Lace, or wrap, and support whole fish
Start it in cold court bouillon
Start smaller, thinner fish in hot court bouillon
Simmer the fish

DON'T: Use vigorously boiling water

II. SEVICHE

DO: Use acid ingredients

III. STEAMING (automatically provides support and freedom from turbulence):

DO: Use acidic ingredients (either on the steamer rack with the fish or in the boiling water)
Keep the steamer vapor-tight

IV. EN PAPILLOTTE

DO: Use an acidic sauce
Make sauce extra-thick
Experiment with the timing

V. BAKING AND BROILING

At high temperatures:
DO: Use a wrapping (vine leaves, corn husks, aluminum foil, etc.) or a coating of other ingredients or bread crumbs
Stuff with high water-content foods

VI. FRYING

DO: Use *hot* oil
Use a coating: flour, breading or batter, especially for deep frying

VII. STORAGE

DO: Keep live saltwater fish in salt water

6

A BOWL OF PLASTIC FRUIT AND THOU

Since life in general is becoming more difficult, it is no surprise that such a seemingly innocent pleasure as eating fruit may be dangerous to your health. Munching an apple in the Garden of Eden had catastrophic consequences, and the same sort of activity today may also alter your future irreversibly. The pesticides that keep the fruit bug-free don't do your body much good, and even a good scrubbing and polishing may not get rid of them. Organic pesticide molecules dissolve in the apple's waxy outer coating, and you have to wash it with *detergent* to render it safe. Depressing.

More depressing is the idea that fruit will never again be as good as it once was. In the country clubs favored by agribusiness executives, the most important decisions are not how to find tastier, more nutritious, and more diverse varieties of foods to grow, but how to grow foods that are easier to pick, package, and ship. Consider tomatoes. Are they grown for flavor, meatiness, or juice? No, they are grown to be tough enough to stand a long truck ride. Moreover, most are picked green; then a simple spray of ethylene gas turns them red.

Ethylene is a fruit hormone produced in the ripening process, but the gassing does not produce the flavor or the vitamins that develop during the natural ripening process. The gassed tomatoes are just as beautiful as naturally ripened ones, but have far less flavor and nutritional value.

So, while our cultural horizons, we are told, are being broadened, our culinary ones are being narrowed. Today there are available to us fewer varieties of apples and potatoes than ever before and fewer naturally ripened fruits.

Of course many fruits continue to ripen after harvesting, but only if they have previously reached a certain degree of maturity. Tomatoes can be mature while still green, and can ripen after picking, but there is no way to distinguish between green immature and green mature tomatoes without cutting them open. Since 80 percent of Florida tomatoes are picked green and gassed, it is a gloomy but foreseeable fact, verified by researchers, that shipments of bright red tomatoes were 40 to 78 percent immature. But the economic advantages are too vast (to harvest green tomatoes, you need go into the fields only a few times a season) to hope the agribusiness boys will repent.

FRUIT JUICES

There is a body of medical opinion that holds that fruit should never be juiced; it should be eaten raw. This arises from the theory that the lack of bulk in our diet is a contributing factor in diseases of the colon. Be that as it may, even the most compulsive health faddist sometimes finds it necessary to prepare fruit juices for dessert sauces, pie fillings, etc. This brings up color problems again, since the pigments in the red-blue fruits are the same class as those in the red-blue vegetables — anthocyanins — and they will also change color as the acidity of the fruit-juice solution changes.

In the next Autodemonstration, you will make some berry juice with acid and with alkali.

AUTODEMONSTRATION L

1 cup strawberries, raspberries, or blackberries
2 cups water
1 tablespoon white vinegar
½ teaspoon bicarbonate of soda (baking soda)

Put the berries and water in a saucepan. Cover and heat to a simmer; simmer for 10 minutes. Drain the juice into 2 glasses. Add the vinegar to one and the bicarb to the other (it will foam — be careful). Compare the colors.

The juice of fruits of this class (apple, blackberry, blueberry, cherry, cranberry, grape, plum, pomegranate, raspberry, strawberry, etc.) will be redder when acidic; purple, blue, green or blue-green when basic. Juices will run a range of colors, and you can make your food redder by including an acidic ingredient like lemon juice.

The next two recipes are similar, but the first has orange and lemon juice, which gives it a strikingly different color from the second, less acidic recipe.

51. RED BLUEBERRY DRINK

(4 cups)

2 cups fresh blueberries
□ 2 cups orange juice
3 tablespoons super-fine sugar
□ 1 tablespoon lemon juice
¼ cup white rum (optional)

Blend everything at high speed in an electric blender for 1 minute.

52. BLUE BLUEBERRY DRINK

(2 cups)

1 cup blueberries
1½ cups milk
2 tablespoons super-fine sugar
1 teaspoon vanilla extract
⅛ cup (2 tablespoons) white rum (optional)

Follow the directions for Recipe 51.

You can play color games by adding or diminishing the lemon juice, or by selecting the right combination of fruits: ripe, sweet fruits with less ripe, and therefore more acidic, ones.

Among these color games is one to avoid: Canned fruit juices, when used to change color on the basis of acidity, can give unexpected results.

AUTODEMONSTRATION M

1 cup blueberries
1 tablespoon pureed *fresh* pineapple
1 cup water
1 tablespoon *canned* (not bottled) pineapple juice

Put the berries and water in a saucepan and boil them, covered, for 10 minutes. Strain the juice and put 2 tablespoons of this juice in each of 3 glasses. Add the fresh pineapple puree to the first glass and the canned pineapple juice to the last. Compare the colors.

The version with the fresh juice is redder than the control, which has no added juice. This is just what we expect, since pineapple is highly acidic. But the sample with canned pineapple juice is quite obviously blue, as though someone had sneaked some alkali into it. Since everyone in your household is honest, that can't be the explanation. The truth is that pineapple juice is acidic enough to dissolve some of the metal from the can.

Dissolved metals are notorious for their reactions with red-blue pigments, usually forming dark blue or even black compounds. Many cans for anthocyanin-colored juices are "enameled" with an interior coating of plastic or ceramic, which protects the metal from attack by the fruit acid. An anthocyanin-based fruit juice will have a low market value if it has the wrong — navy blue — color. But citrus juice cans are rarely packaged this way because the pigments in citrus juices do not react with metals. The noncoated cans can be attacked by acid, but with citrus fruits the evidence of it is less dramatic. Even if the metal dissolves from the can wall into the juice, there is no color change and therefore no untoward marketing effect.

Even if you don't go in for blueberry juice, it is very useful as a sensitive homemade detector of metal in your canned citrus juice. (It has to be sensitive because so little metal actually dissolves, probably much less then could ever be a health hazard.)

These reactions are accelerated by oxygen and it is a good idea to remove unused portions of tomato, pineapple, and citrus products from cans.

Another example of a pigment reaction is the effect of iron on fruit colors:

AUTODEMONSTRATION N

2 fresh strawberries
1 iron, or carbon-steel knife
1 stainless steel knife

Slice one strawberry halfway through with one of the knives, the other with the second knife. Allow the knives to remain between the halves of the strawberries for half an hour at room temperature.

Cut them through and examine the color of the cut flesh.

So avoid metal when preparing fruit dishes, although stainless-steel utensils are all right. If you are storing the fruit preparation for any length of time, it is best to use a glass, ceramic, or plastic container.

BROWNING

A major problem, even in simple fruit dishes, is a color change which does not arise from the fruit pigment, but from the browning of its cut flesh. The browning of meats is a reaction that requires sugar, protein (amino acids), high temperature, and time to develop. The browning reaction that often makes fruit cookery a losing race with the clock is quite a different kettle of apples.

As soon as certain fruits (apples, apricots, avocados, bananas, cherries, figs, grapes, peaches, and pears) are cut or peeled, they start to turn brown at room temperature. (Some fruits are immune: citrus fruits, pineapples, melons, tomatoes, red and black currants, and most berries.) These susceptible fruits contain a compound that turns brown when *oxidized* (when oxygen atoms are added to its structure) and an enzyme that catalyzes the oxidation. The reaction starts when the fruit tissue is cut because it is then able to absorb an enormous amount of oxygen from the air.

The compound is an analogue of *phenol,* also known as carbolic acid. Oxygen adds to these compounds in a sequential fashion until a brown polymer is formed. The enzyme facilitates this addition to these phenols, but is itself unchanged during the reaction. It just speeds the phenol through the oxidation sequence and then is immediately ready to start it over again.

There are only two ways to stop this unaesthetic process: either prevent the absorption of oxygen, or render the enzyme ineffective. The next few recipes illustrate practical ways of following these principles. The first fends off oxygen with a mayonnaise blanket:

53. GUACAMOLE

(2 cups)

2 avocados
1 tomato
½ onion
½ teaspoon chili powder
1 clove garlic, sliced
2 teaspoons lime juice
□ 4 tablespoons mayonnaise, beaten with a fork
1 teaspoon salt
12 black olives
2 pimentos, cut in strips

Cut the avocados in half, remove the pits, and scoop out the flesh.

Peel the tomato (an easy way is to pop it into boiling water for 3 to 5 minutes, then plunge it into cold water to loosen the skin), add it, the avocado, and the remaining ingredients, except the mayonnaise, olives, and pimento, to the blender and blend until quite smooth.

Pour into a bowl, *cover with the mayonnaise,* and garnish with the olives and pimento. Refrigerate for at least 2 hours.

A Waldorf salad works the same way—the dressing acts as a fire blanket to keep oxygen off the sliced apple. In the next recipe this function is served by a syrup.

54. SOUSED FRUITS

- 1 apple, peeled, cored, and diced
- 2 bananas, sliced
- 6 figs, diced
- 6 pears, diced
- 6 peaches, diced
- □ 1 cup powdered super-fine sugar
- □ 2 cups dry white wine
- □ 4 tablespoons white rum

Dissolve the sugar in the wine by thorough stirring. Add the other ingredients and store in a glass or ceramic vessel with a vapor-tight lid.

Refrigerate for a week.

If you are delayed in completing this recipe, just store the cut-up fruits in cold water until you get them coated. French-fry shops use this trick to keep their cut-up potatoes an appetizing white.

Working on enzymes is child's play. Enzymes are so highly tuned and efficient, such sophisticated manipulators of molecules, that any little disturbance will put them off. Like highly strung virtuosi, they cannot do their best in corrosive or sweltering environments. In the Soused Fruits recipe, it is the alcohol that gives the enzyme a hard time. In the next recipe, citrus juice does the same.

55. AVOCADO SALAD

(2 portions)

- 1 avocado
- □ ½ lemon, juice of
- 2 large lettuce leaves
- 1 ounce bleu or roquefort cheese
- 1 small can (3½ ounces/ 99 grams) tuna
- 1 tablespoon mayonnaise
- 1 tomato, sliced
- 12 pitted black olives
- salt

Cut the avocado in half and discard the pit. Sprinkle or brush the cut surfaces with lemon juice.

Place a lettuce leaf on each plate, then add an avocado, cut side up.

Mash the cheese, tuna, and mayonnaise together until smooth and spoon the mixture into the avocados' pit holes. Salt the tomato slices lightly and distribute them and the olives around the avocado.

The *flavor* of the lemon juice is not the primary reason for treating the cut avocados with it. It makes your life more bearable by preventing the avocado surfaces from darkening while you take your time preparing the rest of the salad and waiting for people to sit down for dinner.

All organically active enzymes are proteins and are very sensitive to changes in the acidity of their environment. The activity of a typical food enzyme is at optimum value only in a narrow range of acidity.

Anything acidic will do: citrus juice, apple juice, dressings made with vinegar, etc. The more acidic the covering, the longer the fruit will stay unbrowned.

Enzymes are temperature-sensitive as well and can be inactivated by heat or cold. These are at their optimum efficiency around 100°F; refrigeration will slow the browning somewhat, but cooking will permanently change the enzyme's form, stop its function and prevent browning altogether.

Enzyme activity vs. acidity

AUTODEMONSTRATION O

1 apple
3 tablespoons cooking oil

Heat the oil in a skillet over moderate heat. Slice off one-third of the apple (vertically) and sauté the smaller part, cut side down. When that surface has browned, remove it from the skillet, rinse it in cool water and cut or scrape off the very thin browned layer of cut flesh. Place it near the other part of the apple for 30 minutes, then compare the extent of browning.

BAKING AND BROILING

The one important idea to bear in mind when baking or broiling fruit is the water contained *within* the food. Fruits of high water content will release liquid from the cells as the temperature rises and the cell membranes are destroyed. Unless you are, for some strange reason, after soggy texture (for a dinner party of toothless octogenarians perhaps), the plan of the recipe should be to get rid of or soak up this water.

56. BAKED APPLES

6 firm baking apples (2 ½ – 3 pounds)
□ 1 cup seedless golden raisins
½ teaspoon cinnamon
□ 2 tablespoons sugar
□ 1 teaspoon grated lemon peel
¼ teaspoon nutmeg

Preheat the oven to 375°F.

Core the apple all the way through and *pierce the rest of it with a fork* to provide vent holes. Mix the other ingredients and *fill the cores* with this mixture by placing a finger under the core hole and packing the raisin mixture in tightly from the other side. Fill the hole only 2/3 full.

Set the apples on a *mesh rack* (or aluminum foil pierced all over with a fork) over a pan to collect the drippings. Bake for 45 minutes, or until the apples are *just tender.*

The dried fruit and sugar soak up the water from the inside, and the core and vent holes allow steam to escape from the outside. The mesh holds the apples out of contact with liquid draining from the bottom. In other words, the water doesn't have a chance.

Naturally, if you cook fruit totally immersed in water, if you poach or stew it, the problem of avoiding sogginess becomes more difficult. There is a solution, but to put ourselves in a position to understand it we must first find out about jellies.

JAMS AND JELLIES

Jellymaking is no longer as common in the household as it was just a few years ago. It requires experience and a delicate touch, but can be a quick and satisfying job and worth a few tries.

Pectin is the substance that converts fruit juice to semisolid jelly. It is found as a natural constituent of most fruits, a large negatively charged molecule with many water molecules barnacled onto it.

There are two stages to the jelling process: first, *acid* permits the pectin to change its shape and electrical charge so that *sugar* can then pluck off the water molecules. The unencumbered pectin is then able to link up with other similarly changed and liberated pectin molecules to form the semirigid three-dimensional network.

Pectin contains many carboxylic groups (-COOH), which exist in constant equilibrium with the electrically charged form, carboxylate ($-COO^-$) and with acid (H^+):

$-COOH$	$-COO^-$	+	H^+
carboxylic	*carboxylate*		*acid*
(uncharged)	*(charged)*		

Normally these groups in pectin are in the charged, $-COO^-$, condition, but by adding acid (H^+)—say, lemon juice—the equilibrium is forced to the left, and many of these groups lose their electrical charge. Now the molecule is not so geometrically constrained, and there is less attraction between it and the dangling water molecules. Sugar has a high affinity for water, and strips it off the pectin. All these components must be present: the *pectin* to form the network once the *acid* reduces its charge and the *sugar* dehydrates it.

An easy way to get started is to use commercial pectin. The processor extracts this substance from apple cores and skins or, more recently, from the white substance just inside orange peels. It is an extremely convenient material; with it you can make a jam without any cooking whatsoever.

57. PEACH JAM*

(4½ pounds)

2¾ cups pureed ripe peaches (use a blender)
□ 6½ cups sugar
□ ⅓ cup lemon juice
□ 1 bottle (6 ounces/170 milliliters) liquid pectin

Mix the fruit and sugar and let stand 10 minutes. Mix the lemon juice and pectin in another bowl, then stir into the fruit. Stir for 3 minutes.

Pour quickly into scalded containers, but leave ¼ inch at the top for expansion during freezing. Cover tightly and let set at room temperature (up to 24 hours). Keep in the refrigerator for use within 3 weeks or store in your freezer.

Just a bit of cooking in the recipe will make the jam set much more quickly.

58. STRAWBERRY JAM†

(5 pounds)

3¾ cups pureed ripe strawberries
□ 7 cups sugar
□ ½ bottle (6 ounce/170 milliliter size) liquid pectin
□ ¼ cup lemon juice
paraffin, melted

Mix the fruit, lemon, and sugar in a saucepan and heat to a full boil. Boil for one minute, stirring constantly. Remove from the heat and add the pectin. Skim off the foam and continue stirring and skimming for 5 minutes. Pour into scalded jars and cover with liquid paraffin.

*Recipe courtesy of General Foods Kitchens, Toronto, Ontario.
†Ibid

This illustrates a great molecular principle: *Heat equals speed.* The uncooked jam has to sit around for a day to let the pectins form their network. It takes so long because the molecular collisions are feeble and inefficient at stripping the water off pectin, which then sluggishly bumbles into other pectins and eventually forms a network.

The cooked version, benefiting from high temperature, energetic collisions, quickly prepares the pectins, which then link up much faster.

You can use this technique to prepare really first-class jellies, which ordinarily would require a lot of careful straining through cheesecloth to achieve professional clarity.

59. GRAPE JELLY*

(2½ pounds)

2 cups bottled grape juice
□ 3½ cups sugar
□ ½ bottle (6 ounce/170 milliliter size) liquid pectin
paraffin, melted

Heat the juice and sugar in a large saucepan until it boils, stirring continuously. Stir in the pectin and continue boiling for 1 minute only, still stirring. Remove from heat, skim off the foam, and pour quickly into scalded jars. Cover with liquid paraffin for long-term storage.

The traditional jelly-making technique involves a long cooking period to convert all the pectin-forming substances into pectin. The fruit does this naturally as it ripens, but cooking, particularly if unripe fruit is used, finishes the conversion. Some fruits are endowed with high pectin and acid contents while others are deficient. The following table is not the last word, since the variety and maturity of the fruit is extremely important, too.

*Recipe courtesy of General Foods Kitchens, Toronto, Ontario.

TABLE IV

<table>
<tr><th>High Acid, High Pectin</th><th>Low Acid, High Pectin</th><th>High Acid, Low Pectin</th><th>Low in Both</th></tr>
<tr><td>blackberry</td><td>apple</td><td>apricot</td><td></td></tr>
<tr><td>citrus</td><td>banana</td><td>cherry</td><td>pear</td></tr>
<tr><td>crabapple</td><td>sweet guava</td><td>pineapple</td><td></td></tr>
<tr><td>cranberry</td><td></td><td>raspberry</td><td></td></tr>
<tr><td>currant</td><td></td><td>rhubarb</td><td></td></tr>
<tr><td>tart grape</td><td></td><td>strawberry</td><td></td></tr>
<tr><td>sour guava</td><td></td><td colspan="2">blueberry</td></tr>
<tr><td>loganberry</td><td></td><td colspan="2">fig</td></tr>
<tr><td>plum</td><td></td><td colspan="2">peach</td></tr>
<tr><td>quince</td><td></td><td></td><td></td></tr>
</table>

For fruits low in acid, either lemon juice (or equivalent) or some unripe fruit is added to the recipe. The skins and cores are included in the first cooking step because that is where the fruit localizes its pectin.

Here is a more traditional jam recipe; the pulp will give it some ready-made structure so we can be a bit more relaxed.

60. PRUNE JAM

(about 4 cups)

- □ 1 pound pitted dry prunes
- 2 cups (approx.) water
- □ 1 cup canned crushed pineapple, drained
- □ 2 cups (approx.) sugar
- □ 3 lemons (approx.)
- ½ cup slivered almonds
- paraffin, melted

Cover the prunes with the water and refrigerate overnight. The next day add the pineapple and heat to a simmer. Cook until the fruit is soft. Pulverize in an electric blender and measure the mixture. For each cup add ⅓ to ½ cup of sugar and the juice of 1 lemon. Return the mixture to a saucepan, cover it and place it over low heat.

Simmer until the sugar is dissolved, add the almonds, and cook 20 minutes more, stirring occasionally. Pour into scalded jars and cover with liquid paraffin.

POACHING

We have finally set ourselves up to understand what would seem to be the simplest of fruit-cooking techniques — poaching. When fruit is cooked in plain water, the cell membranes are mangled, osmosis changes, and then the cement that binds the cells to each other falls apart. The result is mush, or more elegantly, puree, and is just the ticket if we want applesauce.

61. APPLESAUCE

(2 – 3 cups)

- 6 apples (2½ – 3 pounds), peeled, cored and sliced
- ½ cup water
- 1 teaspoon cinnamon
- 1 tablespoon sugar
- 2 tablespoons vanilla extract
- 5 tablespoons honey
- ¼ teaspoon salt
- 2 tablespoons lemon juice

Cook the apples in the water until they are soft and the excess water has almost all evaporated. Put the apples and the other ingredients in a blender and puree. Return the sauce to the uncovered saucepan and heat until it is thick.

If you want poached fruit that holds its shape, the sugar goes into the cooking water, and you poach the fruit in a syrup.

62. POACHED PEARS AND ICE CREAM

- 6 firm pears, peeled, cored, and halved
- □ 1 tablespoon lemon juice
- 2 cups water
- □ 2 cups sugar
- □ 2 tablespoons pineapple juice
- ½ teaspoon vanilla extract
- 6 scoops ice cream

Sprinkle lemon juice on the pears to prevent their darkening.

Cook the water, pineapple juice, *and sugar* until dissolved and simmering. Slip the pears *gently* into the syrup and cook carefully until they are just tender (about 10 – 15 minutes). Drain the pears and put them in a bowl. Measure out one cup of the syrup and add the vanilla to it after it has cooled a bit. Pour this over the pears and refrigerate. When chilled, drain again and serve with the ice cream.

Although the stage at which sugar is added in a recipe might seem inconsequential, it is crucial in fruit cookery. Fruits are almost always poached in syrup for a reason more important than slowing the browning reaction and sweetening the dish. It is because sugar firms the texture of the cooked fruit. Sugar serves the same function in poaching as it plays in jelly making — it allies itself with pectin in the formation of a semirigid network.

The sugar localizes at the cell walls of the poaching fruit, where much of the pectin is concentrated. The fruit acid and sugar then push the pectin into a molecular situation where it must cross-link and form a network. This creates a microscopic jelly, located at the cell walls, reinforcing the crumbling structure.

This is the reason fruit canners used to pack everything in a heavy syrup — the syrup helped the fruit maintain a pleasing shape for long shelf life. It is only recently that water-packed canned fruits have become available to calorie-conscious buyers. So the firming effect of heavy syrup is not enormous; you can get away without it if you wish.

Finally, the best way to remind yourself what a lovely thing a piece of fruit can be is to have a fruit tree of your own in the backyard. It is cheaper and more restful than a tennis court or a swimming pool and more beautiful than a parking lot.

CHAPTER 6: RÉSUMÉ

I. WASHING

DO: Use a detergent for waxy fruits

II. COLOR CHANGES OF RED-BLUE FRUITS
(see page 87 for listing)
In acid (Red)
In alkali or when contaminated by metal (Blue)

DO: Keep away from iron utensils

III. BROWNING

DO: Use a coating to keep out the oxygen
Use acid or heat to inactivate the enzyme

IV. BAKING AND BROILING

DO· Use low-water-content stuffings
Pierce the skin

V. JAMS AND JELLIES

DO: Refer to Table IV, page 97, or use commercial pectin
Use sugar and acid
Scald the jars

VI. POACHING

DO: Poach the fruit in water for purees
Poach the fruit in acidified sugar syrup if it is to be served whole

7

SAUCES, CEREAL, PASTA, AND OTHER THICK THINGS: "MAKE IT GOOD AND THICK"

Confronted with the prospect of making sauces, many people panic. Either sauces are associated in their minds with super-refined French cuisine and fancy restaurants, or they've been told too often how difficult sauces are to make, full of phantom lumps ready to materialize at the worst moment. After all, in high-class French restaurants there are full-grown men who do nothing but make sauces, and these *sauciers* are usually second-in-command in the kitchen.

But in reality it is easy to become an absolutely foolproof sauce maker, and you can be one before the end of this chapter. You need only grasp one or two basic ideas (and a wire whisk) to be able to whip up a delicious sauce at a moment's notice.

You needn't even be haunted by morbid thoughts of sagging stomachs or fatty deposits clogging our arteries. For only 30 calories (1 tablespoon cornstarch) and almost no cholesterol, you can thicken a cup of liquid. There is no reason to underachieve gastronomically.

SAUCE

The single most important ingredient in a sauce is self-confidence. After all, preparing a meal shouldn't be like placing a pari-mutuel bet. In the kitchen, the odds should be in *our* favor — and they will be, if we understand how sauces work.

Flour and starch thicken liquids because they have unusual water-absorbing properties. Starch will take up to 25 times its weight of water, absorbing it into its granular structure. These insoluble granules, packed with starch molecules, control the thickening process. As they are heated in water, the bonds between the starch molecules loosen, allowing water to pass into the granule. Latching on to a good thing, the molecular thirst demands more and more water, which sucks up to the individual starch molecules and bloats the granule. The mixture begins to thicken as the swollen granules, like overweight Victorian gentlemen in a narrow hotel corridor, have a hard time passing by each other. When the Big Drink is over, the granules resemble flimsy sacs. At this stage they must be treated gently; severe agitation in the form of overzealous stirring will break up the granules and thin the sauce.

We'll do a few experiments to see how sauce recipes work, and for a modest beginning we'll thicken a cup of water. There is a kitchen utensil that will be very valuable when making these sauces—an empty jar with a cap. I suggest you obtain one now.

AUTODEMONSTRATION P

1 cup cold water
3 tablespoons flour

Heat ¾ cup of water in a saucepan. Put the remaining ¼ cup of water in a jar, add the flour, cap the jar tightly, and shake it well. When the water is boiling in the saucepan, reshake the jar and empty its contents into the saucepan, stirring with a whisk. Reduce the heat and stir gently until the sauce thickens (only a few minutes).

That's all there is to it. This is our prototype sauce, and to get a real one just replace the water with something tasty, like cranberry juice. Using this method, sauce-making is a quick and painless business, and even the shaking maneuver can be fun if you imagine yourself auditioning for barman at the Copa. Before you throw out your experimental results, it pays to taste a minute bit of it if you can bring yourself to do so. If you taste a raw starch flavor, cover the saucepan and simmer the sauce over very low heat for another 2 minutes with occasional stirring. It should then pass the taste test.

The thing to be avoided above all is that obsession of paranoid *sauciers*: The Lump. When the lumps form, the rest of the sauce stays thin, and panic ensues. In the next experiment we'll learn about The Lump.

AUTODEMONSTRATION Q

1 cup cold water
3 tablespoons flour

Heat the water to boiling in a saucepan and add the flour. Stir a bit and let it cook.

Quite a mess, eh? Didn't expect me to do that to you, did you? But now you know about The Lump. Lumps are formed when the starch granules *have not been separated before they start to absorb hot water.* The outer layer of the granule group forms a gooey mass that is impermeable to further water penetration. The granules inside The Lump remain dry, their thickening power is lost, and the sauce stays thin. Not good at all.

Cookbooks have many ways to avoid the dreaded Lump, all of which do only one thing — disperse the granules before the little things see hot water. That's why Autodemonstration P worked. The granules were separated when the flour was mixed with the *cold* water.

Let's start cooking real sauces using this idea.

63. GRAPE SAUCE

(1 cup)

1 cup grape juice, unsweetened
3 teaspoons sugar
□ 3 tablespoons flour

Heat ⅝ cup of the juice and the sugar to simmering in a saucepan.

Put the remaining ⅜ cup of juice in a jar, add the flour, cap it tightly, and shake it well. When the flour is well mixed, add the contents of the jar to the hot juice. Stir continually until the sauce thickens. Cover and cook 2 minutes more over low heat, stirring occasionally.

Remember to shake up the flour-juice mixture *just before* you add it to the hot juice. If it sits around undisturbed for any time, the starch will settle to the bottom of the jar, and it will be undispersed when you add it to the hot juice. And you know what will happen then!

Don't be too athletic when you are stirring the sauce, or those flimsy swollen granule sacs will break up, and the sauce will be thin. Cover the saucepan at the end to cut down on water loss, which causes an ugly "skin" to form.

Let's do it again. Almost any fruit can quickly and with *absolute certainty of success* be turned into an elegant dessert sauce.

64. BLUEBERRY SAUCE

(2 cups)

1 cup blueberries
1 cup water
3 tablespoons sugar
2 tablespoons lemon juice
½ teaspoon cinnamon
□ 3 tablespoons flour

Put the blueberries and ¾ cup water in a saucepan. Add the sugar, lemon juice, and cinnamon. Bring to a simmer and cook for 5 minutes.

Put the remaining ¼ cup water and the flour in a jar, cap it tightly, and shake it vigorously to disperse the flour.

Add the reshaken flour mixture to the simmering blueberry sauce. Stir constantly until the sauce thickens. Reduce the heat, cover, and cook 2 minutes more with occasional stirring.

Excellent! We have a sauce-making method that is marvelous as long as we have some cold liquid to disperse the thickener. But it would be silly to be limited to cold liquids as our starting materials. So let's go on to a second dispersion idea — isolating the granules in a *dry* ingredient of the recipe.

65. ORANGE SAUCE

(1 cup)

□ 4 tablespoons sugar
□ 2½ tablespoons flour
1 cup orange juice
1 teaspoon vanilla extract
2 teaspoons Grand Marnier or other liqueur (optional)

Mix the dry ingredients thoroughly. Heat the juice to simmering in a saucepan, and sprinkle the dry mixture on it, stirring constantly. Reduce the heat, add the other ingredients, cover, and cook 2 minutes more, stirring occasionally.

The flour is sufficiently dispersed in the sugar so that we can add it directly to the hot liquid. The liqueur is added last to keep its flavor in the sauce and not have it vaporized as kitchen deodorizer.

Such sauces are great heretics in the church of gastronomy, because they refuse to admit butter or margarine. These fat-free sauces are ideal for day-to-day use. They can transmute more or less mundane desserts — by which I mean rice pudding, tapioca, sponge cake, ice cream, yogurt, and so on — into an elegant aftermath. If you run out of new "sauce plus something" combinations, vary the temperature. Use a hot sauce on a cold base or vice versa.

It is time I finally get you into trouble. So far our no-worry sauces have been no-worry in preparation and no-worry for health. But now we come to the third of our dispersion techniques — butter-based sauces. When butter appears, the calorie and cholesterol counts zoom. I am a natural worrier, and food has a top position in my fear-and-trembling catalog. But every now and then I have to break out and just eat whatever tastes good. When that happens, I go whole hog and prepare a sauce with butter.

Why is butter so good for sauces? Because, like other fats, it has very little water and can disperse the starch granules, even hot, without lumping them. Any liquid fat will do. Butter gives the most delicate flavor (and the most cholesterol), but you can replace it with margarine without much loss.

66. BÉCHAMEL SAUCE
(1 cup)

- □ 2 tablespoons butter or margarine
- □ 2 tablespoons flour
- ½ cup chicken bouillon
- ½ cup cream
- ¼ teaspoon white pepper
- ¼ teaspoon garlic powder

Melt the butter in a saucepan, then stir in the flour until it is well blended. Add the liquids and pepper, stirring constantly, and cook until the sauce thickens without letting it boil. Reduce the heat, cover, and cook 2 minutes more, stirring occasionally.

This is the famous *roux* ("rue") technique, the classic way to start a sauce by dispersing the thickener in melted fat. Now don't get too worried about the calories and cholesterol. Admittedly I have loaded the deck in this recipe; after all, each tablespoon of butter contains 100 calories and even just ½ cup medium cream has about 360 of those terrible things. But you can modify it easily enough with skim milk instead of the cream and knock the calorie count right down. The cholesterol levels will be thinned out by replacing the butter with margarine. All of a sudden, with margarine and skim milk, you have a sauce that is healthy and delicious, if not as rich as the original version.

This technique is so popular because the melted fat makes an excellent sauce base. The amount of thickener is not as great as in our fat-free sauces, because the fat itself renders the sauce thicker. And of course it tastes smoother and richer. Moreover it makes the sauce opaque, especially with flour as the thickener.

So now you can switch from one to another of our three dispersion techniques (in cold liquids, in dry ingredients, in butter) and among a wide choice of thickeners (check Table V, p. 126) to create your recipe or adapt one from a cookbook to the resources of your pantry.

We have made a number of sauces but have yet to use a common thickener, cornstarch. We must rectify this slight immediately, for cornstarch makes lovely translucent sauces, and since less of it is needed to do the job, it adds fewer calories. For every 2 tablespoons flour (50 calories) you must substitute 1 tablespoon of cornstarch (30 calories). The reason is that flour is not pure starch and doesn't have the same thickening muscle power as cornstarch—it is diluted with calorie-bearing but nonthickening proteins.

Let's now run through a series of sauces, with canned fruit, fresh fruit, and dried fruit, using all three dispersion ideas.

67. QUICK CHERRY SAUCE

(almost 2 cups)

- 1 can (14 ounces/398 milliliters) pitted sweet cherries
- □ 1½ tablespoons cornstarch
- ⅛ teaspoon cinnamon
- ½ teaspoon grated lemon or orange peel

Drain the cherries. The liquid should measure between ¾ and 1 cup. (If it does not, adjust the recipe by adding water if there is too little and cornstarch if there is too much.)

Mix 4 tablespoons of the liquid and the cornstarch in a cup. Heat the remaining liquid in a saucepan with the spice, and when it boils, *stir the starch-water mixture briskly and add to the hot liquid.* Reduce the heat and simmer, stirring constantly, until the sauce thickens. Add the cherries, cover, and simmer, without stirring, for 5 minutes.

The thickener-in-cold-liquid method works well here. In the next recipe we will use fresh tart fruit, so a lot of sugar will be added. Why not switch to the second method, dispersing the thickener in dry ingredients, and use flour again?

68. CHERRY-PINEAPPLE SAUCE
(4 – 4½ cups)

- 2 cups fresh pineapple, pureed in a blender
- 2 cups water (approx.)
- □ ½ cup sugar
- □ 10 tablespoons flour (⅝ cup)
- 4 tablespoons cherry syrup
- 1 tablespoon lemon juice

Mix the sugar and flour thoroughly. Put the cherry syrup and lemon juice into a measuring cup and add water to make a volume of 2 cups. Pour this into a saucepan, heat it just to simmering, and *sprinkle the sugar-flour mixture onto it,* stirring constantly. The sauce will thicken almost immediately. Reduce the heat, add the pineapple puree, cover, and cook 2 minutes more, with occasional stirring.

Now let's try dried fruits using the *roux* technique.

69. APRICOT-RAISIN SAUCE
(3½ – 4 cups)

- 1 package (8 ounces/227 grams) dried apricots
- 1 cup raisins
- 2 cups water
- ½ teaspoon cinnamon
- 2 tablespoons sugar
- □ 4 tablespoons butter
- □ 4 tablespoons flour
- ½ teaspoon vanilla extract

Cook everything but the butter, flour, and vanilla in a covered saucepan for 30 minutes or until the fruits are tender. Reserve and measure the cooking liquid and chop the fruit separately. Dilute the liquid with water to make a volume of 2 cups.

Melt the butter in a saucepan, stir in the flour until it is well blended, and add the cooking liquid. Heat, stirring constantly, until the sauce thickens. Reduce the heat, add the chopped fruit and vanilla, cook 2 to 5 minutes more, covered, stirring occasionally.

Any dried fruit will make a super sauce; it just takes a bit more cooking while the fruit plumps up. Or if you want a smoother sauce, puree the apricots in a blender after they are cooked.

So we can have sauces from juice (or other liquid), canned fruit, fresh fruit, or dried fruit — quite an armory. Now for a few tricks to polish our strategic skills:

BEURRE MANIÉ

Take gravy, for example. If the pan juices have just come out of the oven, we cannot toss in thickener without worrying about lumps. We could, of course, take off ¼ cup of the juices and wait around until it cools so we could make our thickener mixture. But that's a lot of wasted time. Using a *roux* to start is the normal way.

70. GRAVY
(1 cup)

1 cup bouillon (or degreased pan juices diluted with milk, beer, etc., to make 1 cup)
□ 2 tablespoons flour
□ 2 tablespoons butter
salt, pepper, garlic powder, onion powder, to taste

Melt the butter in a saucepan and stir in the flour until it is well blended. Add the hot bouillon or juices, stirring constantly. Reduce the heat and continue to cook, stirring constantly, until the sauce thickens. Cover and cook 2 minutes more, stirring occasionally.

Well, that's not a trick! But if it came out too thin, you would need a trick to thicken the hot gravy. The prospect of starting another *roux* can drive a cook to early retirement. But butter needn't be melted to separate the granules; it can be kneaded. Butter or margarine just warm enough to be pliable can be kneaded with flour to make *beurre manié* ("burr man-yay"), literally "kneaded butter." Shaped into little balls and kept on hand in the refrigerator, *beurre manié* is a cook's salvation. Just toss in a few balls to thicken things up to your viscosity's desire.

Of course, another shortcut, especially if you have concentrated juices, is to disperse some thickener in milk or even tap water and add it to the hot liquids.

BROWNED FLOUR AND ACID SAUCES

If a recipe calls either for browned flour or a lot of acidic ingredients, our rabbit ears should snap up to attention. Maybe only one ear should go up, because browned flour does change things a bit, while the reputed effect of acids on sauces is somewhat exaggerated.

Flour is browned, usually for gravy, because it adds color and flavor. This is done by spreading the flour thinly in a pan and cooking over low heat or in a oven, stirring now and then, until it colors lightly.

The starch part of the flour is being broken down by the dry heat, chopped up into smaller bits. Because of this we must use more thickener (4 tablespoons) than normal (2 tablespoons). The smaller second-generation molecules do not give as much thickening power as their parents. The molecules are all dancing around to the tune of the thermal brass band, vibrating, swirling, and spinning. As the starch molecules in the granule separate from each other and soak up water, their "sphere of influence," the space they appropriate by their whirling-dervish act, becomes larger, as does the granule. The crunch is that a large molecule takes up more space than its smaller descendants.

The decrease in the space that the smaller gyrating molecules occupy is mirrored in the decreased swelling of the granule and the lower thickening power: 50 to 100 percent more flour must be used if it is browned.

Acid has the same effect on starches, particularly flour, which is especially vulnerable. Prove it to yourself.

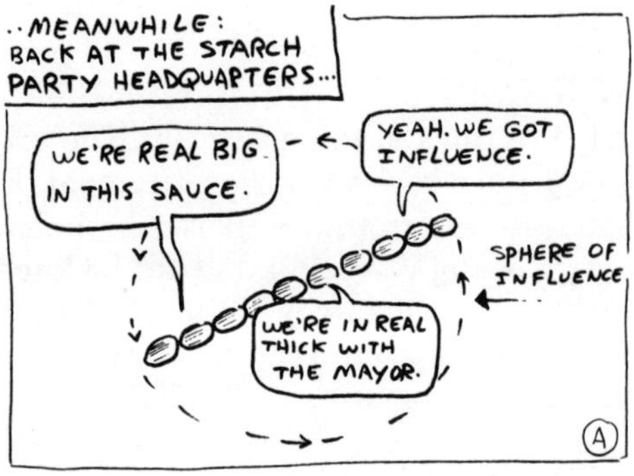

Browning of starch molecules

AUTODEMONSTRATION R

Prepare two flour-thickened sauces:

Acid Sauce

½ cup water
½ cup lemon juice
2 tablespoons flour

Mix the flour in 4 tablespoons of the liquid in a capped jar. Shake vigorously until the mixture is smooth. Heat the remaining liquid in a saucepan almost to boiling, add the flour-water mixture, reduce the heat, and simmer, stirring constantly, until the sauce thickens.

Neutral Sauce

1 cup water
2 tablespoons flour

Repeat the above procedure.

Pour a tablespoon of each sauce onto a piece of waxed paper and tilt it to see how they run.

The acid sauce is obviously looser, so we *do* have a problem. Some cookbooks, tenderly protective, reserve the addition of lemon juice or other acid until after the sauce has thickened. Our fourth experiment will test the necessity of this extra step.

AUTODEMONSTRATION S

4 tablespoons butter
4 tablespoons flour
2 cups water
6 tablespoons vinegar

Melt 2 tablespoons of the butter in each of two saucepans then stir 2 tablespoons of flour into each of them. When it is well blended, add 1 cup water to each *and 3 tablespoons vinegar to the first saucepan only.* Stir constantly until the sauces thicken. Reduce the heat, cover, and cook 2 minutes more, stirring occasionally.

Pour a tablespoon of each sauce onto a piece of waxed paper.

Add the remaining 3 tablespoons of vinegar to the second saucepan and return the two saucepans to the heat. Cook, covered, 2 minutes more.

Pour another tablespoon of each onto the waxed paper. Try the tilt test to compare thicknesses.

In the first set, the acid sauce was thinner than the neutral one—just what we observed in Audodemo R. But the second set showed the two sauces to be equally thin. So the *time* of addition of the acid ingredient did not matter at all.

How can this be? Can all those recipes be mistaken? They can and they are. Decoding cookbooks sometimes involves deleting unnecessary steps.

So don't bother reserving the orange juice for the last step, just beef up the amount of thickener or use some *beurre manié* to compensate for the acidity.

Before we sink into our section on soups, let me urge on you another use of these sauces. A modified fruit sauce can be spooned over leftover duck (or turkey or chicken) to produce an instantaneous, if unauthentic, *Caneton à l'Orange*. Or adapt Recipe 67 and make Duck with Cherries (Duck Montmorency). Good hunting!

SOUPS

Soups can be thought of as thin sauces. Often they are thickened just by the solid matter distributed through them, as in purees. But other times we will have to help them along. Here's a puree recipe that gets helped out with *beurre manié* as the thickening agent. It works fast, and you can get it to exactly the thickness you have in mind by adding the *beurre manié* bit by bit.

71. CREAMED CAULIFLOWER SOUP

- 1 head cauliflower, washed and cut up
- 6 cups chicken bouillon
- □ 2 tablespoons lemon juice
- 2 cups milk
- 4 stalks celery, with leaves, cut in 4-inch lengths
- ½ teaspoon garlic powder
- 1 teaspoon salt
- 2 onions, peeled and sliced
- 2 teaspoons curry powder
- □ 4 tablespoons butter or margarine, softened
- □ 4 tablespoons flour
- 6 tablespoons sour cream
- 6 teaspoons fresh chives, chopped

Cook the cauliflower, celery, onion, and curry powder in the chicken bouillon, *to which the lemon juice has been added.* When the cauliflower is just tender (about 20 minutes), drain the vegetables, reserving 4 cups of the cooking water (add more water or discard some if necessary).

Discard the celery, but puree the cauliflower and onion. Add the pureed vegetables to the reserved cooking water and heat to boiling.

Cream the butter and flour together and add to the hot soup. Cook, stirring constantly, until it thickens. Add the milk and cook 2 minutes more *without boiling.*

Serve hot or cold. Decorate each bowl with 1 tablespoon sour cream and 1 teaspoon chives.

Of course, I wouldn't think of rectifying a thin sauce this way. I would just mix some flour (any thickener will do) with a bit of cold water, and add that to the sauce or soup.

If you have been reading and cooking faster than you have been serving and eating, some of these sauces may now be stored in the fridge, and have jelled into something puddinglike. Actually it's not pudding*like*; it really is pudding. The starch molecules have leaked out of the granules and linked up with others to make bridges. Granules and bridges, all randomly hooked up as though some microscopic city planner had let his demented highway engineer run amok, form a three-dimensional network. The network gives the pudding structural support so it can sit up in the dish. As the pudding/sauce cools, the network traps water to form the semirigid gel that is a pudding. Cornstarch, with long, linear starch molecules, is particularly good at this. Other thickeners, with bushy, branched starch molecules, like overweight dancers with short arms, get in each other's way as they try to link up, and are less suitable for puddings. (The preferred thickeners for puddings are noted in Table VI, *Notes on Thickeners,* on p. 127 at the end of this chapter.)

PUDDING

A youthful, mobile sauce will settle down to a sedentary, solid existence as pudding for the same reason we do — loss of heat and acquisitiveness. Puddings are usually rich enough to contain milk and often eggs as well, so, like rich uncles, they have to be treated gently. But sauce or pudding, the same chemistry is going on, and the same cooking procedures can be used.

72. COCONUT ALMOND PUDDING

- 4 cups milk
- 1 cup dried coconut
- ½ cup sugar
- □ 4 tablespoons cornstarch
- 1 tablespoon almond extract
- 4 tablespoons toasted slivered almonds
- ½ teaspoon cinnamon

Heat the milk with the coconut in a saucepan until it simmers (do not let it boil). Stir the sugar and cornstarch together and sprinkle the mixture on the hot coconut milk with constant stirring, until the pudding thickens. Reduce the heat, stir in the almond extract, cover, and cook 2 minutes more.

Pour into pudding dishes, refrigerate until semisolid, then garnish with almonds and dust with cinnamon. *Cover tightly with plastic* and rechill.

Whenever you heat milk it must be done with great caution or its proteins will scorch. A heavy utensil justifies its high price by smoothing out the heat, eliminating the local hot spots where scorching begins.

When chilling a pudding, cover it tightly with a plastic wrap to cut down on water loss from the surface, the culprit behind "skin" formation. In our recipe, the almonds also served this function.

The next pudding recipe is enriched with eggs, so to avoid ending up with vanilla sauce on scrambled eggs we'll have to take a few precautions.

73. MAPLE RUM PUDDING

(4 cups)

- 4 cups milk
- □ 6½ tablespoons cornstarch
- ½ cup maple syrup
- □ 2 egg yolks, slightly beaten
- 4 tablespoons rum

Mix the cornstarch in ½ cup milk in a capped jar.

Heat remaining milk in a saucepan. When it *simmers* (do *not* let it boil), reshake the cornstarch mixture and add it to the hot milk, stirring constantly.

Mix the egg yolks with the rum in a bowl. *Slowly add ¼ cup of the hot milk mixture, stirring well.* Add another ¼ cup hot milk the same way. Finally, return the entire egg yolk mixture to the saucepan. Add the maple syrup.

Continue stirring until the sauce thickens. Reduce the heat, add the rum, cover, and cook 2 minutes more.

Pour the pudding into serving dishes, *cover tightly with plastic,* and refrigerate.

If egg yolks get hot too fast, they will coagulate, or "curdle." Of course, sooner or later we do have to heat them. So we will do it very slowly, and the trick here is to add a *little* of what is hot to a *lot* of something cool; only small amounts of the hot pudding mixture are mixed with the cool egg yolks until they have been gradually warmed and diluted.

SOUFFLÉ

We are finally in a position to capitalize on our expertise in two areas — egg-white foam, and sauce. Let's combine them to make one of the most elegant preparations possible — the soufflé. A soufflé is just a baked mixture of egg-white foam and a thick sauce.

74. CHOCOLATE ALMOND SOUFFLÉ

- □ 4 tablespoons butter
- □ 4 tablespoons flour
- 1 cup + 2 tablespoons milk
- 2½ tablespoons chocolate syrup
- ⅓ teaspoon almond extract
- □ 4 eggs, separated
- ¼ cup sugar
- □ ¼ teaspoon cream of tartar

Preheat the oven to 350°F.

Melt the butter in a saucepan and stir in the flour until it is all dispersed. Add 1 cup of milk and stir until the sauce thickens. Reduce the heat, stir in the sugar and chocolate syrup until dissolved.

Beat the egg yolks a bit and *slowly* stir 2 tablespoons of the sauce into them, then another 2 tablespoons. Finally return the yolk mixture to the hot milk and stir well. Cook 1 minute more, stirring constantly. Remove from the heat, stir in the almond extract, and let cool at room temperature.

When the sauce is lukewarm, stir in the 2 tablespoons of milk to thin it a bit.

Beat the egg whites with the cream of tartar in a copper, stainless steel, glass, or ceramic (but not plastic or aluminum) bowl until they stand in stiff, but not dry, peaks.

Fold the whites into the chocolate-almond mixture *with a spatula or wooden spoon*. Do half the whites first to lighten the soufflé, then fold in the rest.

Transfer the soufflé *gently* to a 1½- or 2-quart soufflé dish and bake for 40 minutes without opening the oven door.

All the egg-white-foam directions are the same as in the Apple Mousse (Recipe 9, Chapter 1). Fine. We understand that part. Now here are two variations you might want to try:

If you are a culinary overachiever and habitually overbeat your egg whites, producing an unwanted meringue, then a tablespoon of sugar in the egg whites will save you from yourself. Sugar protects proteins so you have to do a lot more beating to denature them. In other words, the sugar extends your margin of error. If you use a hand beater or whisk, save wear and tear on the arm by delaying addition of the sugar until the last part of the beating period.

Salt has the opposite effect, so make all salt additions to the other part of the soufflé recipe, the sauce. This brings us to something else we understand, sauces. For soufflés the sauce should be thick. In this recipe we warm the egg yolks slowly with small portions of the hot sauce, finally using 2 tablespoons of milk to get just the right consistency. Too thin, and the soufflé will fall immediately; too thick, and it won't rise at all. All that's left is to combine the sauce and foam and then bake the soufflé.

The egg whites are folded in with a spatula or wooden spoon to avoid rough handling. It is useful to fold in half the foam first to loosen the structure; the second half will not need as much manipulation to mix in. Then put it into the soufflé dish gently. If you just dump it in, the added weight plopping on top will squeeze the air out of the portion on the bottom.

Now be patient. Keep the oven door closed. The cold draft of your curiosity will chill an undercooked soufflé, and it will sink before your disbelieving eyes. Wait until it is almost done and quickly test by inserting a knife blade with hopes it will come out dry. Even failures can be fun though, for they give you an excuse to eat another soufflé.

Now you can run your sauce-making kitchen your own way. If an arrogant recipe calls for cornstarch when you have run out of it, switch to arrowroot. If you have run out of arrowroot as well, either go shopping or use flour.

Be a master instead of a slave. Read a cookbook for its good ideas about food combinations, but treat its directions about cooking with a grain of salt. For example, most cookbooks will use the butter-flour ("roux") method to make sauces. You can obviously substitute margarine for butter, but why not forget fats altogether and use one of our first two dispersion methods to start the sauce? If a sauce looks interesting, don't let a call for "½ cup heavy cream" put you off; use skim milk (thickened with nonfat dry milk). Of course it won't be as rich, but there are very few recipes where the cream is the major taste sensation. It will be one hell of a lot healthier, and the fact that you are in control will make it taste even better.

CEREAL

One of the more ludicrous defeats for healthy food is our hot breakfast cereals. In keeping with the principle that our cooking is to give us less and less of a sense of accomplishment, most hot cereals are now available in quick-cooking, instant, or faster-than-a-speeding-bullet varieties. The food technologists who produce these culinary miracles have a battery of sophisticated techniques with which to work, but every so often their enthusiasms lead them into a spiral of absurdity.

Old-fashioned hot cereals require 15 minutes to an hour of cooking, so a double boiler or very low heat is used to reduce the scorching hazard. In the days when Scottish students would go off to the university with two sacks, one of apples and the other of oatmeal, as their only nourishment for the semester, the pot of oatmeal was left on the stove overnight.

75. SCOTCH OATMEAL

(4 cups)

1 cup rolled oats (oat flakes)
4 cups water
1½ teaspoons salt
1 tablespoon sugar

Combine the ingredients in a heavy kettle.

Cover tightly and cook overnight in a slow cooker or in a very slow (200°F) oven.

I think it's charming, but I must be wrong because I'm not as rich as General Mills. What they've done to Cream of Wheat (farina) is a good example of modern corporate breakfast philosophy.

It is marketed, by one company, in four forms: 1. "Regular," 15-minute cooking time, containing added iron phosphates; 2. "Quick," 5-minute cooking time, containing added iron phosphate, tricalcium phosphate, and disodium phosphate; 3. "Instant," 30-

second cooking time, containing added iron phosphate and tricalcium phosphate, "enzyme-treated for quicker cooking;" and 4. "Mix 'n Eat," "specially processed farina" to be eaten immediately after mixing with boiling water, with added iron phosphate.

The details of both the enzyme treatment of Instant Cream of Wheat and the special processing of Mix 'n Eat Cream of Wheat are closely guarded as proprietary information. But the functions of the phosphates are typical of the food additive merry-go-round. Iron phosphate is added to all varieties to "enrich" the cereal in iron; but it merely restores to the grain what it has lost in milling. The disodium phosphate is added to the Quick variety because it changes the acidity. The technologists discovered this allowed faster water penetration, and so, quicker cooking. But the human body cannot run on any odd assortment of chemicals; it must maintain a delicate balance between calcium and phosphate. With all that phosphate already added to a staple breakfast food, the harried technologists, forced to restore the "balance," put in yet another additive, one containing calcium: tricalcium phosphate. After all of this doctoring, the food presumably has been reassembled to have a "natural" calcium to phosphate ratio. Catch the iron ring!

If you want a less "refined" breakfast food, why not put together your own?

76. GRANOLA

(4 cups)

3 cups rolled oats (oat flakes)
½ cup wheat germ
½ cup dried coconut
¼ cup honey
3 tablespoons maple syrup
2 tablespoons vanilla extract
1 teaspoon cinnamon

Preheat the oven to 250°F.

Mix everything, and place it on a cookie sheet and bake it for 40 minutes, stirring occasionally, or until the cereal browns.

Cool the mixture, crumble it, and store it in a covered container.

There's not much to be said for North American breakfasts these days. Ready (or not)-to-eat, they contribute little to nutrition or pleasure. A healthy result of the "empty calorie" debate is the marketing of balanced and nutritious, but still "ready-to-eat," dry cereals.

There are other ready-to-eat breakfasts available: cheese and cold meat, fruit salad, herring and onions, etc. Read a travel brochure while you are eating these things, and you may be able to convince yourself that you are Norwegian.

But if your penchant for vicarious travel leads to Asia, you will have to master the cooking of rice.

RICE, PASTA

Rice is the major food staple of over half the world's population. Pasta is steadily increasing in consumption. But does this make cookbooks agree on how to cook them? It does not. Some will have us cook pasta and noodles in oodles of water; others are quite stingy with it. Then some want us to rinse the pasta after cooking, while others throw up their hands in horror over such treatment. Rice cooking also engenders terrible family-destroying arguments.

Just as sauces have their bugaboo in The Lump, so pasta cookery is haunted by the prospect of "sticky noodles." No one wants a spaghetti dish that is more like a bird's nest than a slippery test of fork-and-spoon dexterity. The stickiness is due to the starch that is leached out of the noodles into the cooking water and turns to glue as it cools. One answer is to rinse spaghetti after cooking.

Many people are reluctant to rinse spaghetti, however, perhaps because they are afraid that nutrients will be rinsed off along with the adhering starch. But, alas, by this stage most of the nutrient loss has already happened and rinsing removes only a slight bit more. If you do rinse your pasta, at least use hot water so it will stay warm.

There are two other paths to nonsticky spaghetti. First, you can use a large amount of cooking water. The leached starch will be distributed through a greater volume of water, and the starch solution left on the drained pasta ends up more dilute. Second, you can add a bit (say 1 or 2 tablespoons per quart of cooking water) of oil, margarine or some other fat. It coats the noodles and makes it impossible for the starch to attach itself. It also has the nice side effect of preventing the cooking water from foaming over. (Remember that just a little fat killed our egg-white foam.) If you cook pasta this way you may not even have to add any more fat when serving it, and you can safely let it sit around a few moments while you work on another part of your recipe.

77. SPAGHETTI DANIELI

1½ pounds spaghetti
6 quarts water
3 tablespoons salt
□ 3 tablespoons olive oil
1 pound prosciutto, cut up
3 tablespoons butter
2 egg yolks
1½ cups cream
Parmesan cheese

Fill a large pot with the water, salt, and olive oil and bring to a boil. Add the spaghetti. Keep tasting strands of the spaghetti; when it is cooked *al dente* (with a bit of resistance when bitten through), drain it thoroughly.

Melt the butter in a large skillet and sauté the prosciutto for 5 minutes. Add ½ cup of cream, mix thoroughly, and add the cooked, drained spaghetti to the skillet.

Mix the egg yolks with the remaining cup of cream and stir it into the mixture. Cook 3 to 5 minutes. Serve with Parmesan cheese.

Polished rice is a different story. "Enriched" varieties have had successive layers of nutrients coated on the grains. Even converted rice, which has been parboiled to drive nutrients from the exterior bran into the interior of the grain before the bran is polished off, leaves most of them close to the surface.

Almost all rice recipes that you find on boxes insist you cook the grains in the minimum amount of water; when no water is poured off, no nutrients can be lost. That seemed like a clever idea, but then the overworked food technologists had to go back and solve the problem of gummy rice. This was done by genetic engineering on the rice to develop a strain that did not leak out much of its starch. Like Cream of Wheat, there is a sort of Rube Goldberg improvisation to the thing. We start off with something that works—brown rice—and modify it (polishing) for nonessential, even frivolous reasons, little realizing that each modification leads in unforeseen ways to others, all trying to restore the original qualities.

Food habits are among the most intransigent of attitudes. Immigrants will assimilate language and religion long before they adopt new kinds of food. Asian recipients of enriched rice supplied by an aid program refused the stuff, because the enrichments had colored the rice yellow. They would only be happy with pure white rice. North Americans are no better in this respect; rice that cooks up with a yellowish tinge may face rejection. If yours does this, it is most likely because your cooking water is hard and alkaline. A bit of lemon juice in the cooking water (1 tablespoon lemon juice in 4 cups of water) will neutralize the water and whiten up your rice.

If you don't want to use preprocessed (instant) rice — and who can blame you — here's an alternative:

78. RICE

1 cup white rice, regular
□ 2 – 2½ cups *rich* chicken bouillon
(add ½ tablespoon butter if the bouillon is lean)
(short-grain rice requires a bit less liquid than long grain)
□ 1 teaspoon lemon juice

Boil the bouillon and lemon juice, then stir in the rice. Cover and cook for 25 minutes. Stir occasionally to prevent scorching.

If the rice is too moist, remove the cover for the last 10 minutes of cooking and stir it regularly.

The fat is for "separate grain" enthusiasts. It does the same job on rice grains as it did on pasta — lubrication. The oil on the rice grains repels the water and starch molecules, and we take advantage of their molecular hostility.

EMULSIFIED SAUCES

Sometimes in making sauces we want to take advantage of peace and harmony. French dressing, mayonnaise, hollandaise, and béarnaise sauces are formed of liquids that ordinarily would find each other repellent. Oil and vinegar, for example, really do not want to mix, but are brought into harmonious union by the beneficent actions of a chemical matchmaker, the emulsifier.

Even in their final form these sauces contain liquids that are just barely able to hide their mutual lack of affection. If allowed, one partner will retreat into narcissism, form small solitary droplets, and drift unconcernedly throughout the other. Their natural inclination is to club together, get out of that inhospitable other liquid, by forming one *big* drop. The emulsifier's function is to keep these droplets small and dispersed, and it does this by the traditional matchmaker's device of presenting a different face to each partner.

Oil and water do not mix because their electrical characters are different. Oil is composed of nonpolar molecules, whose electrical distribution is uniform, but water is quite polar, with the oxygen part of the molecule negatively charged, and the hydrogen parts positively charged.

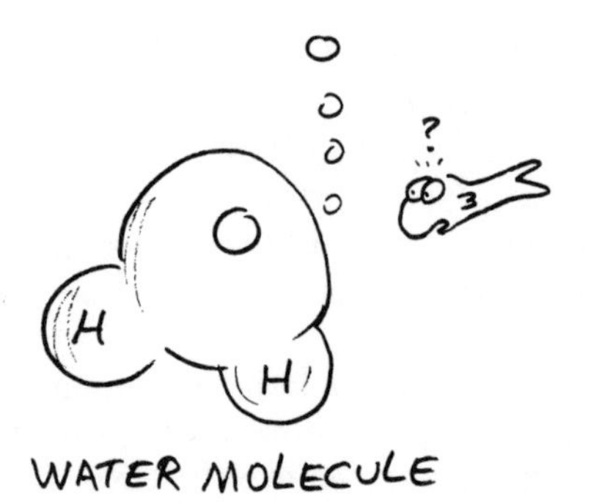

WATER MOLECULE

Emulsifiers are molecules that are partly polar and partly nonpolar.

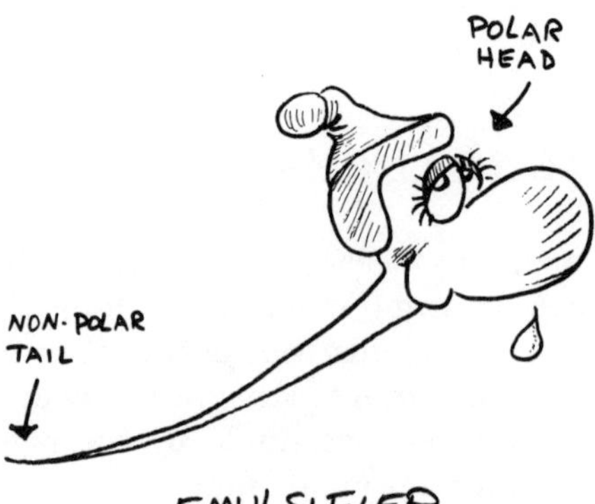

EMULSIFIER

The nonpolar part of the emulsifier dissolves in the nonpolar oil globule, and the polar head sticks out.

Emulsifier in action

Now the nonpolar oil has donned an encircling mask of emulsifiers and appears, *from the outside*, to be a big *polar* molecule. As such, it is welcomed into the polar water and dissolved in it. Some emulsifiers are not so perfectly designed for their job; paprika and dry mustard help stabilize French dressing temporarily by collecting at the droplet surfaces. Other such sauces are helped to hang together by honey, cooked sugar syrup, or a large amount of dry ingredients, which thicken the sauce merely by making it more viscous. The droplets then find it hard to move around, find each other, and coalesce.

79. SALAD DRESSING
(about 1 cup)

□ 1 cup olive oil	1 clove garlic, minced
□ 3 tablespoons fresh lemon juice	½ teaspoon oregano
½ teaspoon salt	½ teaspoon dill
½ teaspoon pepper	□ 1 tablespoon honey

Combine all the ingredients in a blender and blend at moderate speed for 20 seconds. Let stand for an hour or two, momentarily re-blend, and serve.

A mixture of olive oil, lemon juice, and garlic (just a weakly seasoned French dressing) produces only a temporary emulsion. But in this recipe the honey thickens the dressing so you don't have to go into your bartender's act again during dinner.

Of all the natural polar-nonpolar emulsifiers, lecithin, the one present in egg yolk, is best. Egg yolk is always the mark of a classy sauce. It makes the sauce smooth and allows it to be rich, with a lot of oil or butter held in the water-based sauce. But the oil-holding capacity of any sauce is limited. If too much oil is used in making mayonnaise, it "breaks," and the oil forms a separate layer. The cure for broken mayonnaise is to change the concentrations of the ingredients so there is either more emulsifier (egg yolk) or more water or vinegar in which to disperse the oil.

Every cookbook I have found in which it explains how to repair broken mayonnaise has been very strict: "Do not add egg yolk, water, or vinegar to the broken mayonnaise; add a little bit of the broken mayonnaise to a beaten egg yolk and continue adding and mixing bit by bit." But as a registered iconoclast, I had to try the forbidden recipe. It was frustratingly true; an egg yolk dropped into broken mayonnaise disappeared like a rock in a pond and the oil layer still lay there, separate. It was demeaning, but necessary, to follow directions, especially after I convinced myself they were rational. At first it seemed that this simple reversal of order had more to do with magic than chemistry, but it really is not done with mirrors. Broken mayonnaise is added slowly to the egg yolk because emulsifying is easier with a high lecithin concentration. A little bit of mayonnaise in an egg yolk is just slightly diluted egg yolk, so it is very high in lecithin, much higher than the mayonnaise. The reverse, though, one egg yolk in a jar of mayonnaise, increases the lecithin concentration only a bit.

It is the same pseudo-magical principle when water or vinegar is used to re-form the emulsion. It is easy to emulsify a few drops of mayonnaise in water or vinegar because the oil concentration is so low that the droplets are well separated and find it hard to coalesce.

Mayonnaise is easy to make at home, especially with a blender.

80. MAYONNAISE

(about 1½ cups)

- □ 1 cup olive oil
- □ 2½ tablespoons vinegar
- □ 1 teaspoon ground mustard
- ½ teaspoon salt
- ½ teaspoon pepper
- 1 clove garlic, minced
- □ 2 egg yolks

Put ½ cup olive oil in a blender, add the other ingredients, and blend slowly. Add the remaining oil while the blender is on. Do not continue blending once the dressing has become uniform.

All the directions conform to the same principle—keep the egg (and lecithin) concentration as high as possible as long as possible. The oil is added in stages, and slowly, so the emulsion can be started with a high proportion of egg.

Mayo's close relatives in the same family, hollandaise and béarnaise, are a bit more difficult because they are heated.

81. MANUAL HOLLANDAISE SAUCE

(1 cup)

- □ ¾ cup butter, melted but not hot
- □ 2 tablespoons lemon juice
- □ 3 egg yolks, slightly beaten
- ¼ teaspoon salt
- ½ teaspoon white pepper

Heat *only ¼ cup butter with the egg yolks* in a *double boiler* over hot water that is *just below the simmering point.* Stir constantly until the sauce thickens. *Slowly* add the rest of the butter, bit by bit, stirring constantly. Add the lemon juice, salt, and pepper.

Cook and stir a few minutes more until the sauce appears well blended.

A recipe for béarnaise sauce would be the same except that vinegar and herbs replace the lemon juice and salt. Of the two things that can go wrong with these recipes, overcooking the yolk is the most potentially disastrous. If this happens, the egg curdles, and you can kiss that sauce good-bye, unless you are brave enough to serve egg-drop sauce with steak.

The other potential failure, also a result of too much cooking, is separation because of loss of water. If the water content gets too low, the barrier between the oil droplets is insufficient, and they slide together to form an oil layer. The cure is simple. Replace the water that has been lost by evaporation by adding a tablespoon or two of water to the sauce and stirring it in.

A simpler way to avoid these problems is to use a blender to prepare hollandaise and béarnaise. The quality is only slightly lower.

82. MECHANICAL HOLLANDAISE SAUCE

(about 1 cup)

- □ ¾ cup butter, melted and *hot*
- □ 3 egg yolks
- □ 2 tablespoons lemon juice
- ¼ teaspoon salt
- ½ teaspoon white pepper

Put the egg yolks, lemon juice, and seasoning into a blender. Turn it on to low speed and add the butter *slowly*. Serve immediately or store, tightly covered, in the refrigerator.

TABLE V

Substitutions for Thickeners

For every 2 tablespoons of flour, substitute:

4 tablespoons browned flour
1 tablespoon cornstarch
2½ teaspoons arrowroot
1 tablespoon tapioca (quick cooking, granulated)
1 tablespoon potato starch
2½ teaspoons rice flour or rice starch
(3 teaspoons = 1 tablespoon)

TABLE VI
Notes on Thickeners

Thickener	*Resistance to thinning when overcooked*	*Gel formation*	*Comments*
Wheat flour (all-purpose)	Poor	Fair	Does not freeze well
Cornstarch	Good	Good	Does not freeze well
Arrowroot	Good	Fair	Does not reheat well
Tapioca	Fair to Poor	Poor	Freezes well
Potato starch	Fair	Poor	
Rice flour	Good	Poor	Freezes well

CHAPTER 7: RÉSUMÉ

I. SAUCE

DO: Prepare sauces in one of these four ways:
(a) disperse the thickener in a small amount of cold liquid and add it to hot or cold liquid; or
(b) disperse the thickener in dry solids and add it to hot or cold liquid; or
(c) disperse the thickener in liquid fat and combine with hot or cold liquid; or
(d) disperse the thickener in plastic fat by kneading or creaming them together and combine with hot or cold liquid
Use a capped jar to prepare a flour + water dispersion

DON'T: Add undispersed thickener to hot water or water-based liquids

II. PASTA AND RICE

DO: Cook pasta in a large volume of water with 1 – 2 tablespoons of fat per quart of cooking water
Use fat and lemon juice when cooking rice

III. MAYONNAISE, etc. (egg-emulsified sauces)

DO: Keep the egg concentration high

DON'T: Overcook
Allow excessive water loss

8

DESSERTS: IT COMES WITH THE MEAL

Desserts are like props of a science-fiction movie—magic potions that transform the body into unlovely forms. Double chins, pot bellies, and big bottoms led a prior existence as sherbet, ice cream, and candy. As a member of the formerly fat fraternity, I feel that eating a dessert is a sinful act and punishment will soon follow—which it does, when I weigh myself.

But there *are* special occasions, and some desserts are low enough in calories to be guilt-free, even in daily use. Some of the best are custards and gelatins.

CUSTARDS AND GELATINS

Fruit jellies jell by forming a three-dimensional network of the carbohydrate, pectin. Custards and gelatins are semifirm because they also build a supporting network, but with a different kind of molecule—proteins. Although the final structures look similar, the materials of construction are different, and different cooking techniques are used to hook the molecules together.

CUSTARD

In the case of custard, the network is formed by proteins from egg. The thickening proceeds just as it would in other forms of egg cookery—the egg proteins unfolding and rejoining under the influence of the thermal, acid, and salt environment. The end result is either a stirred custard — a thick sauce used on cake, ice cream, and fruit — or a more solid and independent baked custard. To see if we are paying attention, cookbooks often call stirred custard "boiled custard." This is particularly inventive of them since this custard must not boil.

83. STIRRED WINE CUSTARD

(about 3 cups)

- □ 8 egg yolks
- ⅓ cup sugar
- 2 cups of milk
- 2 tablespoons port, Madeira or Marsala wine

Beat the egg yolks and sugar together until they are well mixed, then mix in the milk. Heat the mixture in a *double boiler, stirring constantly.*

When the custard coats a spoon, add the wine, stir it in, and remove from the heat.

Stirring is absolutely essential. It hinders the network formation, breaks up the structure, and prevents it from becoming extensive; the custard thickens but does not become semirigid. The stirring gives a "pourable" custard. It does not create firmness — it prevents overfirmness.

If you refuse to stir, you will end up with two preparations in the double boiler. The bottom of the mixture will have absorbed all the heat, so the top of it will still be uncooked, and you can pour it into a glass and then down the drain. What remains is custard, but unpourable and difficult to serve. Belated stirring at this point will yield something with the right thickness but the wrong texture — too many lumps where the structure has formed solidly enough to survive the stirring.

Alcohol-based flavorings are added after the cooking; added too early they will be vaporized and lost. The milk need not be scalded although that does shorten the cooking and stirring time. Scalding is a holdover from the days before commercial pasteurization, but is necessary to extract the flavor when a vanilla bean is used instead of vanilla extract.

84. STIRRED VANILLA CUSTARD
(about 3 cups)

□ 6 egg yolks
⅓ cup sugar
□ 2 cups milk
□ 1 vanilla bean

Heat the milk and vanilla bean in a saucepan just to *simmering.* (Do not let it boil.) Remove it from the heat, cover it, and let it stand 30 minutes. Then discard the bean.

Beat the egg yolks and sugar together until they are well mixed, then stir in the cooled vanilla milk. Heat the mixture *in a double boiler, stirring constantly.*

When the custard coats a spoon and does not drip, quickly remove it from the heat.

Since the milk may be somewhat warm when added to the eggs, it is done with stirring so the yolks warm gradually. Use a double boiler to prevent curdling, which will produce scrambled egg in your custard.

In some custard recipes, not only is it unnecessary to *scald* milk—you can dispense with it altogether!

85. ZABAGLIONE (MARSALA CUSTARD)
(½ cup)

□ 6 egg yolks
4 tablespoons Marsala wine (or other dessert wine)
4 tablespoons sugar

Beat the sugar into the egg yolks and stir in the wine. Heat over a *barely simmering double boiler,* stirring continually.

Since there are no milk proteins to help the thickening, the recipe's proportions have to be changed; in this case there are more yolks per cup of liquid.

These custards are stirred to keep them smooth, but when they bake, undisturbed, the network forms and the custard becomes firm.

86. BAKED CUSTARD

- □ 4 eggs
- □ 4 egg yolks
- ⅓ cup honey
- 3 cups milk
- 1 tablespoon lemon peel, grated fine
- 3 tablespoons grated chocolate
- 1 teaspoon cinnamon

Preheat the oven to 325°F.

Beat the egg, egg yolks, and honey together until just well mixed. Stir in the milk and pour into custard cups or dishes. *Set them in a pan of water* ½ inch deep, cover with some aluminum foil, and bake for about 45 minutes.

Test the custard for doneness by inserting a cake tester (or other thin metal object) *a bit off-center* into the custard. When it comes out clean, remove the custards from the oven and sprinkle grated chocolate and cinnamon over them.

Serve the custards in their baking dishes.

This recipe starts off like Stirred Vanilla Custard, Recipe 84, but since there is no vanilla bean to heat, the milk can be added all at once to the eggs. Then the custard containers are set into a pan of hot water and covered. The pan of water acts as an insulator; although the oven is at 325°F, the water cannot get hotter than 212°F, the boiling point at sea level. This is a nice slow way to bake, and the cover, perhaps just a sheet of aluminum foil, reflects just enough heat to prevent the top from drying out or scorching. (By the way, when stirring the milk, be a bit lazy; if you beat it too much, air bubbles will make the custard porous.)

Custard is very sensitive to the baking temperature, so the water insulator is very important, as can be seen in the following Autodemonstration.

AUTODEMONSTRATION T

2 eggs
2 egg yolks
1½ cups milk

Preheat the oven to 325°F.

Beat the eggs and egg yolks together until well mixed. Stir in the milk and pour the mixture into 2 or more custard cups, all of the same size and material. Set half the cups in a pan of hot water about ½ inch deep (as in Recipe 86), but put the remainder on a bare oven rack. Bake both sets simultaneously until done according to the knife test.

The texture and even the color of the two will be vastly different. The insulated batch will have a much smoother texture, which comes about from the slower, evener cooking. The other set of custards will be porous and much less tender. Overcooking makes too many bonds between the network molecules, which tightens the network and squeezes out liquid, an unpleasant sight called "weeping." This is the reason the knife test is made *near* the center but not *at* it. The heat held in the custard and the cup will continue the cooking after removal from the oven and is enough to finish cooking the center.

Many alterations can be made in a custard, which will not only give a different taste, but will change the texture. Increasing the proportion of eggs will increase firmness, because there is more protein available to form the network. Conversely, diluting the egg with a lot of milk will give a softer custard. Acid ingredients (fruits, molasses, honey) help denature egg proteins (Chapter 1), so whatever protein is available is more efficiently utilized to give a firmer network, whereas sugar protects the proteins from denaturation (Chapter 7, Soufflés) and gives a softer structure.

Because egg whites denature at a lower temperature than yolks, the whites cook very easily into a network. A high proportion of whites to yolks will therefore give a firmer product.

TABLE VII
Texture of Baked Custard

Firmer	*Softer*
High proportion of eggs	Low proportion of eggs
Less liquid	Dilution (e.g., with milk)
High proportion of egg white	High proportion of egg yolk
Acid ingredients (fruit, molasses, honey, cream of tartar)	High sugar content

If you have found a recipe with a *texture* you like, but you still want the freedom to change its taste from time to time, play both sides of the table. For example, if you want to prepare a custard for a cholesterol-conscious eater, the replacement of several yolks by whites could be offset by adding a bit more sugar or milk.

For custard pie, firmness is most helpful. The usual problem with custard pie fillings is that they manage to get the crust soggy before they set. The remedy is to choose ingredients that make a firm-textured custard, since they set more quickly than the softer ones. This is one of the few instances where scalding the milk will actually do some good. In this case it shortens the time the custard remains liquid and cuts down on the leakage.

GELATIN

Recipes with delicate textures (mousse, custard) will often shorten the odds by including gelatin to help make a stable structure. This recipe uses gelatin to firm a mousse made with beaten egg whites rather than whipped cream. You should be such an egg-white-foam expert by this time that we won't pass a single comment about it.

87. STRAWBERRY MOUSSE

- □ 1½ envelopes (¼ ounces/7 grams per envelope) unflavored gelatin
- 1 cup orange juice
- ½ cup sugar
- 2 cups strawberries
- ½ teaspoon vanilla extract
- ½ tablespoon Grand Marnier or other orange-flavored liqueur (optional)
- □ 2 egg whites
- □ ⅛ teaspoon cream of tartar

Sprinkle the gelatin over ¾ cup juice and let stand 5 minutes. Meanwhile puree the strawberries with the remaining ¼ cup juice. Heat the gelatin mixture slowly until all the crystals are dissolved. Add the puree and sugar, and heat to simmering. Remove from the heat, add the vanilla and liqueur, and refrigerate until it begins to thicken.

Beat the egg whites with the cream of tartar in a copper, stainless steel, glass, or ceramic (but not plastic or aluminum) bowl until they stand in stiff, but not dry, peaks.

Fold the whites gently into the gelatin mixture *with a spatula or wooden spoon.* Refrigerate *at once* for 1 hour, or until the mousse has set.

Timing is critical if you want uniform texture. Lack of patience might lead you to mix in the egg whites before the gelatin has started to firm. Once hidden in the fridge, it will take revenge by separating into a lighter egg white layer over a heavy gelatin. (This will still be edible and even attractive.)

Here is another example of gelatin as a backup.

88. PINEAPPLE CUSTARD

□ 4 egg yolks
¼ cup sugar
□ 2 cups milk
□ 1 envelope (¼ ounce/ 7 grams) unflavored gelatin
□ 1 cup *canned* crushed pineapple, drained

Beat the egg yolks with the sugar until well mixed. Sprinkle the gelatin onto the milk and let it stand 5 minutes, then pour it into the egg-sugar mixture. Heat this mixture *in a double boiler, stirring constantly*. When the custard coats a spoon, remove the mixture quickly from the heat. When it has cooled to lukewarm, stir in the pineapple, pour into serving dishes, *cover tightly*, and refrigerate.

The network formed by gelatin is composed of animal protein. Gelatin, extacted from mammalian bones and hide, is really just purified glue. When softened in cold water, it swells slightly and disperses. At high temperature, the molecules unhook and then reassemble during cooling to form the network.

Now what if you have no canned pineapple, but there is a nice fresh one sitting around? Is an innocuous substitution of fresh for canned pineapple a good idea? Here's a test.

AUTODEMONSTRATION U

2 cups pineapple juice (canned)
1 envelope (¼ ounce/7 grams) unflavored gelatin
1 small fresh pineapple

Sprinkle the envelope of gelatin onto the pineapple juice in a saucepan, place it over low heat, and stir constantly until the gelatin dissolves (until no granules are visible, about 3 minutes). Remove from heat and pour into 2 dishes or bowls.

Take the meat from the pineapple and blend it to a puree or chop it as finely as possible. Put *one tablespoon* of the puree into *one* of the dishes of gelatin.

Chill both gelatin preparations overnight in the refrigerator.

In the morning the preparation without fresh pineapple will have jelled and when tipped will not budge; the one with it will still be liquid and sloshable.

Fresh pineapple ruins the scenario *not* because it is acidic — canned pineapple juice is just as acidic — but because fresh pineapple is a good meat tenderizer.

There are enzymes in pineapple (and figs and papaya as well) that cut up protein molecules and break down whatever molecular protein structure they encounter. Since gelatin is a protein, these enzymes go right to work and scissor up the molecular bonds. So none of these fruits can be used in gelatins fresh. If you refuse to use canned substitutes, the solution is to *poach the fruit*. The high temperature destroys the enzymes just as canning would do, and the gelatin proteins can form their structure in peace and harmony.

There may be times when your desire for a gelatin requires instant gratification. Ice or a frozen ingredient will hasten the jelling.

89. FAST BOUNCY GELATIN

(3 cups)

□ 1 package (3 ounces/ 85 grams) *flavored* gelatin
¾ cup boiling water
½ cup cold water
□ 1 small can (6¼ ounces/178 milliliters) frozen fruit juice
1 tray ice cubes

Put the gelatin in a mixing bowl and mix in the boiling water until the gelatin is dissolved. Add the frozen juice and cold water. Stir until the juice is dissolved. Add the ice cubes and beat with an electric mixer until the ice is melted. Refrigerate.

But just a moment! What about the cold-water-gelatin-softening ritual? This recipe just throws it right into boiling water. But *this* recipe calls for *flavored* gelatin, which is a mixture of gelatin, sugar, fruit, acids, flavors, and coloring. The gelatin is already dispersed in dry ingredients and won't lump when put into hot water. Gelatin cookery uses the same tricks as sauce cookery for preventing starch lumps: dispersal or premixing.

The use of ice or frozen ingredients will speed up the jelling, but we have to pay for it, for the result is less stable than one that forms slowly in the refrigerator. Day-old gelatin is even more stable (more cross-links and bonds have formed in the structure), so if you expect the gelatin dish to stand around in a hot room when served, prepare it a day or so ahead and keep it well chilled.

CANDY

As a reformed fatty, I have not eaten candy for quite a while, and cooking it is a personal nutritional heresy. But it is a real treat for others at celebrations or on holidays. And, although it is not the easiest kind of cookery to master, requiring some practice and even luck, the science governing it is pretty simple.

Confectionery depends on sugar cookery — forming sugar solutions and controlling sugar crystallization. Syrup cooking has traditionally been dominated by subjective "soft ball, hard ball" tests, which are fine for the experienced cook. But most of us will be better off using a candy thermometer. The point that may be unclear is why a sugar syrup should be cooked to the precise temperatures usually given in candy recipes. It is because the concentration of the syrup determines the character of the candy, and there is a direct connection between the concentration of a sugar solution and its boiling temperatures.

As the syrup boils, water is lost by evaporation, and the syrup becomes more concentrated. A salt solution boils at a higher temperature than pure water, and so will any solution of water and dissolved solids. As the concentration of dissolved sugar molecules increases, they interact more and more with the water molecules, making it more difficult for them to vaporize. Since more energy is required to reach boiling, the temperature of the boiling point is higher. So each temperature of boiling syrup is associated with a unique sugar concentration. For example, the creamy center of many candies is made from fondant, and it is boiled until the temperature reaches 236–238°F; at this temperature the candy has arrived at the proper sugar concentration, and we can proceed with the rest of the recipe. Temperature is being used as an indicator of concentration.

Check out your analytical instruments before you go to work. If your thermometer reads anything other than 212°F (100°C) in boiling water at sea level, you are in jeopardy. At high altitude the boiling temperature will read less than this. To avoid ambiguity, I will specify boiling points as the number of degrees above the normal (sea level) boiling point. For example, 232°F will be specified as "20°F (11°C) above the normal boiling point."

The next stage of candymaking is the cooling of the syrup. In the simplest cases, creamy candies like fondant, fudge, and divinity, the cooling syrup forms myriads of extremely small sugar crystals. The trick is to keep the crystals small; if they get too big, the otherwise creamy candy will have a grainy texture and a gritty taste. So these candies contain, besides sugar and water or milk, some ingredients that prevent graininess; either □ corn syrup or □ cream of tartar, or both. These □ ingredients inhibit the formation of large crystals, but in different ways.

Corn syrup is mostly glucose and is quite different from granulated table sugar, which is sucrose. They are not equally sweet, they have different solubilities, and they do not fit into each other's crystal structures.

It is as if you had borrowed your kid's building blocks to build a solid cube, but had to fit in some 11-sided blocks left by a passing extraterrestrial. They will not fit, and if they are forced in, the structure collapses. The mixture of sugars hinders the crystal formation of either one, so corn syrup can add *sweetness*, without adding to the tendency for sucrose to crystallize.

Cream of tartar acts in a completely different way. Sucrose, when dissolved in water and heated with an acid, such as cream of tartar, breaks up into two simpler sugars, one of which is glucose.

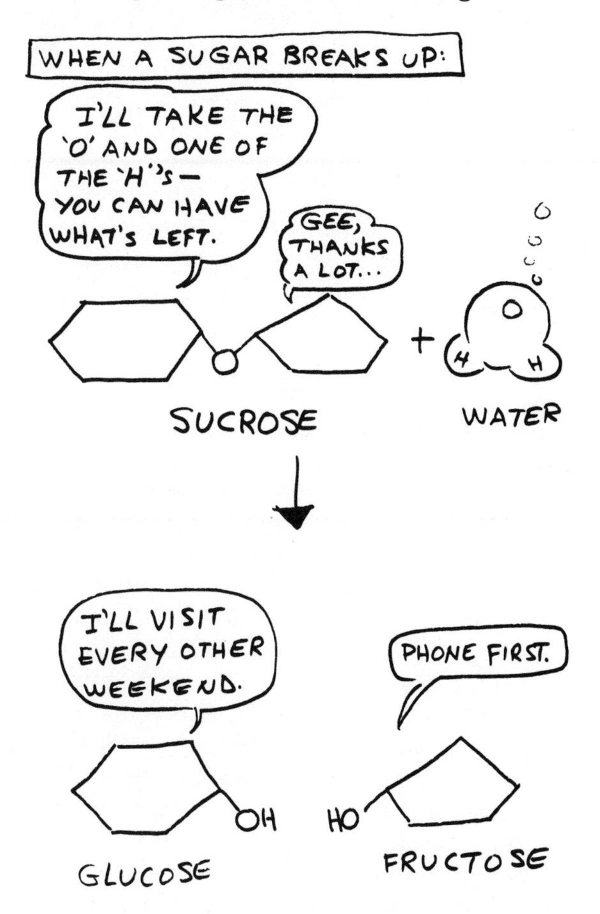

The reaction is called *inversion*, and the glucose-fructose mixture is called invert sugar. The usefulness of this reaction is twofold: it reduces the sucrose concentration, decreasing its tendency to crystallize, and it produces invert sugar, which is highly soluble and resists crystallization.

Fudge is just slightly less simple than fondant. It adds milk (perhaps evaporated), butter, and quite often chocolate. The milk and butter add flavor and richness, but they also function by inhibiting graininess. These ingredients attach to and coat small sugar crystals and prevent their further growth. Now here's my fudge recipe, which is so careful it includes all of these helpers: corn syrup, cream of tartar, milk, and butter.

90. CHOCOLATE ALMOND FUDGE

(24 1-inch squares)

- □ 1 cup milk
- 2 squares (2 ounces/ 56 grams) unsweetened chocolate
- □ 2 cups sugar
- □ 1 tablespoon corn syrup
- □ 1/16 teaspoon cream of tartar
- □ 2½ tablespoons butter, cut up
- 1 teaspoon almond extract

Cut up the chocolate and add it to the milk in a heavy saucepan or kettle. Heat slowly, stirring constantly, until the chocolate is dissolved. Mix in the sugar, corn syrup, and cream of tartar, and stir until the sugar has dissolved and the mixture is smooth. *Using a damp pastry brush, wash any remaining sugar crystals down from the insides of the pan.* Cook, *uncovered, stirring occasionally with a wooden spoon until a candy thermometer reads 238°F (114°C), or 26°F (14°C) above the normal boiling temperature.* (Another check on your thermometer is to drop a bit of the syrup into very cold water; at this concentration it can be formed into a soft ball in the water.)

Remove the pan from the heat, add the butter *without stirring*, and let the mixture cool. When it is lukewarm (about 115°F or 46°C), add the almond extract and beat the mixture until it thickens. Without scraping the sides of the pan, pour the mixture into a greased 9-inch square (or round) pan and score it in squares. Cool thoroughly in the refrigerator and cut through the scorings to make fudge squares.

If the fudge refuses to harden, warm it in hot water, return it to the saucepan with a few tablespoons of water and bring it slowly up to boiling again. When it reaches the appropriate temperature, proceed as in the preceding paragraph.

Most of the cooking directions aim to prevent premature crystallization. As the fudge cools, the tendency to crystallization increases — the velocity of the molecular impacts keeping the molecules apart gets smaller — until finally the molecules can attach to each other, and the whole system starts to crystallize all at once. This means that it is happening all through the fudge at innumerable centers and that the final crystals will be small, just what we want. But if the crystallization starts too early, many fewer crystals start to form, and each one can grow much larger. This can be started accidentally by a small object, even dust, dropped on to the surface, or by too much movement, and very easily by an undissolved sugar crystal. So we are carefully instructed to wipe them away with a damp pastry brush. (Some recipes cover and cook the sugar solution for a few minutes to do the same thing. Steam condenses on the interior of the pan and washes down any crystals that have collected there.)

Stirring is avoided to prevent crystallization; so is scraping the pan — the former to avoid movement, the latter, sugar crystals.

Finally, a word about the holy wooden spoon. It is a pretty nifty item. It will not mark a pot or discolor the candy, it doesn't make much noise when stirring, but more important, it is a very poor conductor of heat so it will not become uncomfortable while you are working hot candy. And wooden spoons are cheap.

The final beating is not to harden the fudge — cooling does that — but to start crystallization in as many places as possible so they will all be small.

When a sugar solution is cooked to a higher temperature and a higher concentration, more and more stringent measures are needed to avoid premature crystallization. Acid ingredients become more important and the proportion of corn syrup is increased. This becomes most important when making candies that should have no crystals at all: caramel, toffee, taffy, and brittle.

The syrup for peanut brittle is even thicker. It is concentrated until it boils at 300°F (149°C), or 88°F (49°C) above the normal boiling point. Some syrup dropped into very cold water at this stage will form a hard thin sheet (hard crack). It is one of the most concentrated syrups you will have to deal with, so to prevent crystallization it has the highest proportion of corn syrup to sugar. But the temperature, which up to now has just been an indicator of the syrup concentration, begins to play a role of its own. At such a high temperature, the sugars break down to produce new flavor compounds and a brown color; they caramelize. What is more, some acids are produced, and when an alkali, like baking soda, is added, the acid and the alkali neutralize each other and, like a fire extinguisher, give off gaseous carbon dioxide, CO_2, which makes the mixture foam and produces a light texture.

91. PEANUT BRITTLE
(about 2 pounds)

- □ 2 cups (1 pound) sugar
- □ 1 cup corn syrup
- ¾ cup water
- □ 4 tablespoons butter
- □ ½ teaspoon baking soda
- 2 cups unsalted roasted peanuts
- ½ cup ground unsalted roasted peanuts

Cook the sugar, syrup, water, and butter in a heavy kettle until the sugar is dissolved. *Cover* and cook 10 minutes, then *uncover and continue cooking without stirring, until a candy thermometer reads 300°F (149°C),* or 88°F (49°C) above the normal boiling point.

Add the nuts, stirring them in with a *wooden spoon*, add the baking soda and stir. The candy should bubble. Pour it onto a greased working surface (a cookie sheet) as quickly as possible and shape it into a ½-inch-thick slab. Mark it in squares and let it cool, then cut the squares apart and store them in a covered container.

The recipe hopes that the sugar will not scorch, which is caramelization carried too far. But when it works, caramelization is a beautiful finishing touch, as in this showy custard dessert, crème brûlée.

92. CRÈME BRÛIÉE

- □ ¾ cup brown sugar (approx.)

Make any custard or pudding (pages 113 – 115, 129 – 134) in ovenproof dishes and have them thoroughly chilled. Cover the surface of the puddings with brown sugar (about 2 tablespoons to each pudding), and *set them in a tray of cold water* ½ inch to 1 inch deep. Place the tray and puddings under the broiler (or salamander) until the sugar starts to burn. Serve immediately, but don't burn your lips — it's hot!

The trick of protecting the custard with a cold-water bath is easier than it sounds, and the results are flamboyant.

ICE CREAM AND SHERBET

Now that ice is in the picture, homemade ice cream is the next item to snarl our diet plans. Most commercial products have artificial flavorings, as well as a host of strange-sounding additives to smooth the texture. No matter what your feelings about additives, the choice of commercial flavors, limited and mostly artificial, is enough to make homemade ice cream worth trying.

Ice cream was invented long before the mechanical refrigerator. What made that possible was the fact that water can be frozen at a temperature lower than 32°F. The same molecular process that makes solutions of salt water or sugar boil at temperatures higher than 212°F forces them to freeze at temperatures lower than 32°F. The salt or sugar interferes with the crystal-forming process, messing up the water molecules' orderly beginnings of crystal nuclei, just the way sucrose and glucose foul up each others' crystals. This, coupled with the energy from the molecular collisions, is enough to break up every opportunity to crystallize. The only way to force the solution to freeze is to decrease the effect of the collisions, that is, to lower the temperature.

So when I make ice cream — that is, when I freeze a fairly concentrated sugar solution — it must happen at a temperature less than 32°F, typically 25°F. The freezing medium, the salt-ice-water mixture, must also be concentrated, for it must be even colder than this. There is a continual balance to be maintained — if the ice cream is made more concentrated, so must the brine.

A friend of mine was making ice cream for a group and couldn't get it to harden. He thought some more crank-turning was necessary — probably in accordance with the idea that when something goes wrong, it is always the most difficult remedy that is the necessary one. All he needed to do was throw some more salt into the freezing brine; the temperature would have fallen immediately as long as there was sufficient ice. I was too bashful to point this out to my laboring friend, and as a result I ended up drinking my ice cream.

But when the temperature is low enough for freezing, we must cope with another problem, one that we faced making candy — large crystals.

In candy, there were sugar crystals to worry about; in ice cream there are ice crystals. If they grow too large, the texture will be gritty. This eighteenth-century recipe sets out the rudiments of ice-cream making and contains some primitive attempts at crystal control.

To Make Ice Cream

Pare, stone and scald twelve ripe apricots, beat them fine in a marble mortar, put to them 6 oz. of double refined sugar, a pint of scalding cream, work it through a hair sieve, put it into a tin that has a closed cover, set it in a tub of ice broken small and a large quantity of salt put amongst it, when you see the cream grow thick around the edge of your tin, stir it, and set it in again till it grows quite thick, when your cream is all frozen up take it out of your tin, and put it into the mould you intend it to be turned out of, then put on the lid, and have ready another tub with ice and salt in as before, put your mould in the middle, and lay your ice under and cover it, let it stand 4 or 5 hours, dip your tin in warm water when you turn it out; if it be summer, you must not turn it out till the moment you want it: you may use any sort of fruit if you have no apricots, only observe to work it fine.*

This mix is very simple: fruit, sugar, and cream. Scalding the cream in those prepasteurization days was good preventive folk medicine, and it still is, since low temperatures do not kill pathogenic bacteria, and they feed and grow on ice cream even better than we do.

The brine is prepared, but the mix is not stirred until the cream has thickened. This was just common sense at a time when churning was an everyday experience and the recipe was for apricot ice cream, not apricot butter, which might result from agitating a rich, warm mix. When the mix starts to thicken, it has cooled, and stirring can start without fear of butter production.

A nice pause before beating, perhaps even a cocktail, is a good idea, if only to concentrate our resolve for this boring and taxing job. But why is stirring necessary? Certainly not just to get uniformity; a couple of revolutions (of the stirrer) would do that. Stirring or beating is required because one of the pleasures of ice cream is a smooth and airy texture, and it is the beating that produces it by breaking up large ice crystals and incorporating air, a great deal of air. Ice cream

*Elizabeth Whitaker Raffald, *The Experienced English Housekeeper,* London, 1789.

freezers are filled to less than two-thirds of capacity because the air beaten into it will increase the volume about 50 percent. Here is a modern rendition of this eighteenth-century recipe, using a metal can for good heat transfer from the cream to the brine:

93. OLD-FASHIONED APRICOT ICE CREAM

(2 quarts)

12 apricots
½ cup milk
2 cups cream
¾ cup sugar
□ 10 pounds ice, crushed
□ 3 cups rock salt (or 2 cups table salt)

Stone the apricots and puree them with the milk in an electric blender until smooth. The puree should measure about 3 cups. Heat the cream and sugar until it is dissolved. Do not let the mixture boil. Put the cream in the refrigerator until it has cooled, then mix in the puree.

Pour the cream into a *metal* can. (If you have a commercial freezer, put it into the inner can and fit it with the paddle.) Make sure that the can is *no more than two-thirds full.* Set the covered can into a bucket (the freezer bucket) and pour in a 2-inch layer of ice between the freezer bucket and the can. Then sprinkle in 3 tablespoons salt. Continue filling the space between the can and bucket alternately with ice and salt.

Start churning immediately and continue until it is hard to turn or the motor stalls (about 20 to 30 minutes). The ice cream will have the consistency of thick mush. Pack it into containers, leaving ½ inch at the top for expansion during further freezing, and harden the ice cream in your freezer for 2 hours before serving.

Modern ice cream recipes, like the ones on the next few pages, are basically the same. They usually have more ingredients, but these are mainly to improve the texture and to keep that texture during storage.

94. RICH VANILLA PEACH ICE CREAM
(4 quarts)

- 1 quart milk
- 3 cups cream (or another 3 cups of milk)
- □ 2 vanilla beans
- □ 1¾ cups sugar
- ¼ teaspoon salt
- □ 6 tablespoons flour
- □ 6 egg yolks, lightly beaten
- 4 ripe peaches, peeled, stoned and pureed (about 3 cups)
- □ 10 pounds ice, crushed
- □ 3 cups rock salt (or 2 cups table salt)

Mix the sugar, flour, and salt.

Heat the milk and vanilla beans in a saucepan just to simmering. (Do not let it boil.) Add the sugar mixture and cook, *stirring constantly,* at the *simmer* until the sauce thickens. Mix the yolks with the cream and add to the sauce. Stir in the peach puree. Continue heating until the entire mixture is hot but not boiling. Remove from the heat and cool in the refrigerator. Discard the vanilla beans.

Pour the cream into a *metal* can. (If you have a commercial freezer, put it into the inner can and fit it with the paddle.) Make sure that the can is *no more than two-thirds full*. Set the covered can into a bucket (the freezer bucket) and pour in a 2-inch layer of ice between the freezer bucket and the can. Then sprinkle in 3 tablespoons salt. Continue filling the space between the can and bucket alternately with ice and salt.

Start churning immediately and continue until it is hard to turn or the motor stalls (about 20 to 30 minutes). The ice cream will have the consistency of thick mush. Pack into containers, leaving ½ inch at the top for expansion during further freezing, and harden the ice cream in your freezer for 2 hours before serving.

The egg yolk, as usual, is very important because its lecithin helps emulsify the butterfat so the sauce won't separate. The more fat, the less the ice-crystal problem, for the fat coats the crystals and prevents their growth. The flour also helps this way by soaking up a great deal of excess water as it gelatinizes and thickens.

One of the promises I made for homemade ice cream was the chance to use unusual flavors. Fresh fruits are especially tasty in ice cream, but most recipes will, as is the case in Recipe 93, puree them. The problem with large pieces of fruit is expense — one might have to buy a plastic tooth to replace one broken on a fruit chunk that has been frozen to rocky hardness. Fruit does this because it is full of water in the form of a rather dilute solution and will freeze at temperatures just below 32°F; that is, it will freeze *before* the ice cream, which does so at 25°F. Nice soft pieces of fresh fruit in an ice cream are a rare delight, but someone discovered a trick — soak them in a syrup.

95. FRESH FRUIT ICE CREAM

1 cup fresh strawberies, *sliced*
□ ⅔ cup sugar

Mix the sugar and strawberries and let stand overnight in the refrigerator.

Make any ice cream and stir in the strawberry mixture just as you pack it into containers for hardening in the freezer.

This charming device is very simple — water in the fruit is extracted into the concentrated syrup. In its quest for water molecules, the thirsty sugar solution drains the fruit tissues. Some of the sugar also diffuses into the fruit. The solutions in the fruit become more concentrated and therefore freeze at a much lower temperature — lower, we hope, than the ice cream. If you don't have enough time to follow this recipe, frozen strawberries are an excellent alternative, sitting as they are in a ready-made heavy syrup.

Now what if your apartment or budget is too small for an ice cream freezer? Then just use the freezer compartment of the refrigerator. You will have to do a little work breaking up the ice crystals and puffing in the air, and the recipe had better help you out.

96. COFFEE ICE CREAM
(1 – 1½ quarts)

1 cup milk
1 cup cream
2 cups double-strength coffee
□ 1 cup sugar
□ 4 eggs yolks, slightly beaten
□ 3 tablespoons flour
⅛ teaspoon salt
1 tablespoon coffee liqueur
1 teaspoon vanilla extract
□ 4 egg whites
□ ⅛ teaspoon cream of tartar

Mix the sugar, flour and salt.

Heat the milk, cream, and coffee in a saucepan and add the sugar mixture. Cook at the *simmer, stirring constantly,* until the sauce thickens.

Remove from the heat, slowly stir ¼ cup of the sauce into the yolks, then another ¼ cup, and finally return the yolk mixture to the sauce. Cook it 5 minutes more, stirring constantly, remove from the heat, and stir in the liqueur and vanilla. Put it in the freezer compartment until it is mushy.

Beat the egg whites and cream of tartar in a *copper, stainless steel, glass, or ceramic (but not plastic or aluminum)* bowl until they stand in stiff, but not dry, peaks. *Fold* them gently into the ice cream mush *with a spatula or wooden spoon.* Freeze the ice cream until it is hard.

The foam-making ingredient, egg white, is beaten *separately*, and then folded in. Whipped cream or milk will also supply the missing air, and gelatin will help preserve the airy structure by setting quickly.

Sometimes—often in the case of fruit flavors—homemade ice cream or sherbet will fail to harden. To counteract the fruit's natural tartness, more sugar is put into the mix. But this makes the mix more concentrated, and the temperature at which it freezes is lowered. So we just set the freezer compartment for its lowest temperature, or put some more rock salt into the brine to harden the ice cream. But when it comes out, it doesn't seem to have enough flavor because our taste buds become less sensitive as the food gets colder. So the next time we put more tart fruit (and more sugar) in the mix, and the temperature has to be lowered even more. This descending spiral is not as bad as it sounds, but it explains why fruit sherbets and ices do not get as hard as ice cream in the freezer.

A word of caution at this point. If you are convinced that ice cream making is a worthwhile investment of time and money, do not expect the result to behave like commercial ice cream. All those additives serve to keep the texture smooth during long storage and the hardness within strict limits. The homemade variety will be harder in the freezer and softer in the dish. Its crystal structure will be less stable, tending, over time, to graininess, so it should be prepared in small batches that can be finished up during the week or on the spot.

The dieters who have not fainted partway through this chapter, and who are waiting for some kind of low-calorie word, have even more bad news in store. When I was dieting, the usual escape hatch was ice milk or sherbet. This was an ego boost, as well, since I could slurp up my ice milk while gloating over my puritanical rejection of the nearby ice cream. But that was all illusion. Although ice milk has fewer calories than ice cream pound for pound, it also has less air incorporated into it. Comparable portions are served up in equal volumes, like scoops. And since the air deficiency makes ice milk denser than ice cream, it has almost the same caloric content, scoop for scoop.

Is fruit sherbet our salvation? Not likely. It has even less air than ice milk, and because of the fruit tartness has much more sugar. The average caloric value of all these are within 15 percent of one another. Big deal.

Are the dieters still there? There may still be an answer for them — miracle fruit.

This is an extraordinary South American fruit that has the property of making sour foods, eaten subsequent to it, taste sweet. The fruit has been commercially extracted to produce a pill, which is chewed a few minutes before eating a "sweet" grapefruit or lemon! It might seem fitting that a science-fictionlike development is needed to counter the deep and abiding passions some of us hold for sweets. Unfortunately the laws of retribution rarely miss — the FDA has just banned this substance in the United States until further tests are done.

CHAPTER 8: RÉSUMÉ

I. *CUSTARD*

A. Stirred Custard

DO:	Stir continuously
DON'T:	Boil Add alcohol-based flavorings early in the cooking

B. Baked Custard

DO:	Use a pan of water as an insulator when baking Make the knife test off-center
DON'T:	Stir too much while mixing

C. Custard Pie

DO: Make a firm custard
Use gelatin as a last resort

D. Change custard textures by following Table VII on page 133

II. GELATIN

DO: Soften in cold water (with unflavored gelatin)

DON'T: Use *fresh* pineapple, fig, or papaya
Serve *freshly made* gelatin or one *made with ice* on a hot day

III. CANDY

DO: Include more crystallization preventers in the more concentrated candies. These preventers are acid ingredients (cream of tartar, honey, molasses, lemon juice, etc.), corn syrup, milk, and butter
Beat well after cooling

DON'T: Stir or move the pan while cooling
Allow dust to fall in it (use a cover)
Allow buildup of sugar crystals on the inside of the pan (wipe off with a damp cloth or cover the pot to steam them off)

IV. ICE CREAM

DO: Allow the mix to cool before stirring
Add more *salt* to chill the ice water if the ice cream doesn't harden
Add more egg yolk or flour to the next attempt if you want to improve the texture

DON'T: Scald the milk (it's optional)
Fill the mixer more than two-thirds full
Include pieces of fruit without presoaking them in syrup

9

BAKING: "IF IT'S ENRICHED, IT NEEDS ENRICHMENT"

BREAD

Of all the seductive and irresistible odors that waft our way, that of freshly baked bread takes a top spot on my list. I will loiter in bakeries, nostrils distended, until it becomes embarrassing. My dieter's willpower will shrink and disappear if a loaf of bread is served fresh from the oven. My nose will take over the controls.

This remarkable odor is such an elusive, transient property that it still has not been pinned down chemically. So the best way to get a good sniff is to do our own baking. But breadmaking is so different from most forms of cooking that there is a psychological barrier to overcome. We will surmount it in little steps — the first being breads that have no leavening.

UNLEAVENED BREAD

The first executive chef of unleavened bread was probably Moses, and we still cook some of these flatbreads in ways not much different from his recipe. One of the most popular in the Western Hemisphere is the tortilla. Here is a version that uses flour in place of the usual cornmeal.

97. WHEAT-FLOUR TORTILLAS
(12 tortillas)

- □ 2 cups all-purpose flour
- □ ¼ cup butter
- □ 1 cup water
- ½ teaspoon salt

Preheat the oven to 350°F.

Mix the ingredients, *knead only to blend* — for *about 1 minute*. (If the dough falls apart, use more water.) Let stand 15 minutes.

Divide the dough into 12 parts and roll each part out to form a disk.

Bake on a greased cookie sheet or grill on a frying pan until just brown, about 2 minutes, then turn and brown the other side.

Flour, especially wheat flour, has unique properties, which man exploited by inventing kneading. Why is this step necessary in bread-making? What does it do to the dough?

Wheat flour contains 5 – 15 percent protein, but the word "protein" does not describe a single entity. There are many different protein molecules that, while they may have many properties in common, are each unique, with idiosyncratic behaviors.

Two of the many protein species in wheat flour, when allowed to soak up water, become unpleasant to handle. Gliadin ("glee-ah-din") becomes gluey, and glutenin ("gloo-ten-in") becomes rubbery, but if they are hydrated and simultaneously forced into each other's molecular neighborhood, they bond together to form an extraordinary compound — gluten.

Like the beautiful child of ordinary parents, gluten is a blend of the most useful properties of its components. It is cohesive, forming a three-dimensional structure that holds the dough together, and it is also elastic, so the dough can stretch and expand. Flatbread is flat not only because it is unleavened, but also because it is rolled into a thin sheet of dough for quick cooking with a minimum of fuel. If there is not enough kneading, and consequently insufficient gluten, the dough is difficult to roll and handle; it tears, and sticks to anything — rolling pin, board, hands, face, floor, children. . . .

On the other hand, overkneaded dough develops so much gluten that the bread turns out rubbery rather than chewy. Too much gluten, and the dough snaps back like a rubber band every time you try to roll it out. Some recipes, even for flatbreads, include an antirubber ingredient, fat.

Butter or shortening coats the embryonic strands of gluten, waterproofing them and thus preventing their further growth. Shortening is so named because it shortens the gluten strands, and keeps the dough manageable. Our tortilla recipe works two ways: kneading to make gluten, shortening to keep it under control.

PIE PASTRY

Water, dough, and handling produce gluten. Shortening hinders it, so does minimum water and minimum handling. These principles govern the making of pie pastry. I am partial to tough, gummy, elastic pastry, easy to make and with desirable appetite-losing properties. But I have had it pointed out to me, with fine delicacy, that this is an aberration born of sloth and guilt. So I have tried to understand the hocus-pocus and incantations of pie-pastry recipes.

98. PIE PASTRY

(2 9-inch shells)

- □ 2½ cups all-purpose flour
- 1 teaspoon salt
- □ 5–7 tablespoons (approx.) *ice* water
- □ ¾ cup (1½ sticks) butter, shortening, or lard, *chilled*

Chill a mixing bowl, 2 knives (or a pastry blender), a fork, and a rolling pin.

Sift the flour with the salt into the chilled bowl, *cut in* the shortening *with the chilled knives or blender* until the dough looks mealy.

Blend in the ice water, bit by bit, *with the chilled fork* until the dough hangs together when squeezed. Put it in the freezer for 15 minutes.

Roll it out with the chilled rolling pin, using a little flour on the working surface.

These directions are pretty bizarre — chilled bowl, working with cold knives and forks, ice water, chilling the dough — but our Holmesian deductive powers will decode them.

What does a fanatical piemaker want? Flaky crust. How does he get it? By making a dough with just enough gluten so that it will roll out without tearing and by building into it thin layers of insoluble fat. As the crust bakes, the fat layer melts and releases water and air, which vaporize into blisters of steam, separating the dough into flakes. The last direction ensures a few more fat layers, a few more flakes.

Those other directions are legitimate because this recipe is single-minded about flakiness and therefore about keeping everything cold. (A richer recipe, with more shortening, would give us less work in preparation, but more in dieting.) The colder and harder the shortening, the less opportunity the flakes of shortening have to liquefy and disappear into the dough. The knife and fork routine is to prevent me from heating up the dough by sticking my hot little fingers into it. And being so cumbersome, the utensils also prevent a lot of dough-toughening manipulation. Using ice water keeps the temperature down for flakiness, and using as little of it as possible discourages gluten formation, also for tenderness.

Tenderness is not the property most evident in unleavened breads. But technology has always served luxury, and in time yeast leavening was developed by the ancient Egyptians. Molar-cracking flatbreads were transformed into rich, airy loaves.

YEAST DOUGH

The most dramatic effect yeast has on baking is gas liberation, as it ferments sugar into gaseous carbon dioxide and ethyl alcohol.

glucose (a sugar) *(yeast)* *carbon dioxide* (CO_2) + *ethyl alcohol*

The expanding CO_2 makes the dough rise, forming innumerable tiny pockets of gas "cells," which enlarge during baking.

99. WHITE BREAD

(2 9-inch × 5-inch loaves)

- □ ½ cup *warm* water (105 – 115°F/40 – 46°C)
- □ 1 teaspoon sugar
- □ 1 package (8 grams) dry yeast
- 1 cup milk
- ⅔ cup *hot* water
- □ 1 tablespoon butter or margarine
- □ 2 tablespoons sugar
- □ 1 tablespoon salt
- □ 6 cups all-purpose flour

Do not preheat your oven yet! But warm up your first mixing bowl.

(a) *Activating the yeast:* Put the warm water (it should feel warm, but not hot, when tested on the inside of your wrist), the yeast, and 1 teaspoon sugar in the bowl. Stir until well mixed. Let it stand 10 minutes.

(b) *Dissolving the other ingredients:* In another mixing bowl combine the milk, the ⅔ cup of hot water, the butter, the rest of the sugar, and the salt. When well mixed, stir up the yeast mixture and add it in.

(c) *Mixing:* Mix in half the flour, gradually, then the rest. If the dough sticks to the bowl, add a bit more flour. Gather up the dough on a working surface and let it rest 10 minutes. It should feel soft but not sticky.

(d) *Kneading:* Knead the dough on a floured surface until it becomes smooth and just a bit elastic (but not rubbery). This should require 5 to 10 minutes of work.

(e) *First Rising: Grease* a bowl and put the dough in it. Cover with a *damp* towel and place in a warm part of the kitchen (80°F) for about 1½ hours, or until it has risen to double its original size. (Set in a sink with a few inches of warm water if your kitchen is cold.)

(f) *Punching:* Punch down the dough with a well-washed fist. Divide it in two and shape into smooth loaves. Pinch the seams closed with your fingers.

(g) *Second rising:* Grease two dark metal bread pans and place the loaves in them. Put them in the same warm spot (80°F) for another hour — or until double in bulk. *Now* preheat the oven to 375°F.

(h) *Baking:* Bake for 30 to 40 minutes or until the top is brown and the bread slips easily from the pans.

This is a very efficient recipe; there is no wasted effort. The yeast must be hydrated in water that is neither lackadaisical nor enthusiastic. Too cool and a dough-harming substance diffuses out of the yeast; too hot and the yeast gives up with heat prostration and stops fermenting. The next step should proceed at the same temperature. The boiling water will heat the milk enough so that stirring a bit cools it to lukewarm (110°F).

Old recipes call for scalding the milk, and this was necessary when unpasturized milk was in common use. Gluten development is hindered by proteins found in raw milk, but the heat treatment of pasteurization denatures these special proteins and eliminates the problem. Nowadays scalding is *unnecessary* (unless you are one of those very few people with access to unpasteurized milk), but convenient. A lukewarm mixture will melt the shortening, dissolve the sugar and salt quickly, and speed up the mixing.

It would be liberating to eliminate the two and a quarter hours the dough sits around fermenting, but these dinner-delaying risings are required to produce lots of gas cells. If bread dough is baked just after kneading, before the yeast has worked, a little monstrosity will result. Such a loaf will be very compact because the yeast has not had time to loosen the gluten structure, and then died from the heat before it could give off much gas. It will look and taste like a big biscuit.

Punching the dough after the first rising forces out excess CO_2 and subdivides the gas cells so the texture will be light and airy. If I let the dough rise too much, the gluten overstretches and the structure weakens. The cells become large and the texture coarse. Even though it does not taste like the bread properly prepared, it is pleasant. Moral: Disasters of preparation may still delight the persevering.

Greasing the dough and bowl holds down evaporative loss of water, as does the towel and draft-free environment, and prevents dry-crusting of the surface.

At high altitude, there is less atmospheric pressure pushing down on the dough, so the amount of leavening is reduced. Otherwise, "doubling in bulk" may happen so fast that the other chemical interactions that accompany fermentation (for instance, a gentle softening of gluten) can't get started.

An older recipe illustrates once again the mind-boggling ability of tradition to precede science.

100. POTATO BREAD

(2 9-inch × 5-inch loaves)

- □ 2 potatoes, peeled and cut up
- □ 1 package (8 grams) dry yeast
- 1 cup milk, scalded
- 1 tablespoon butter
- 2 tablespoons sugar
- 1 tablespoon salt
- 4½ cups all-purpose flour

Cook the potatoes in boiling water for 40 minutes, or until they are soft. *Reserve ½ cup of the cooking water* and discard the rest. Puree the potatoes in a blender, keeping only ¾ of a cup.

When the cooking water has *cooled down to about 110°F* (warm on the inside of the wrist), put it in a warm bowl with the yeast. Stir and let stand 10 minutes, then stir again.

In another mixing bowl, dissolve the butter, sugar, and salt in the hot milk. Cool to lukewarm, then mix in the pureed potatoes and the yeast mixture.

Follow directions **(c)** through **(h)** of Recipe 99, White Bread.

Why on earth did they save the potato-cooking water and then use it to start the yeast? Is there any good reason for this part of the recipe? The chemical answer turns out to be astonishing.

Yeast, of course, transforms sugar into gas for leaven. But in doughs that are not sweet there may not be enough sugar around to provide an adequate supply. Yeast is a finicky eater; it wants only glucose and won't eat sucrose, table sugar. However, yeast is an animal with inner resources. It contains enzymes (similar to those in our saliva) that can break down sucrose or starch into simpler sugars, glucose among them. So yeast can manufacture its food even from starch, but the amazing thing is that it can do it most easily with potato starch. The potato-cooking water, loaded with potato starch, is a particularly digestible food for the yeast, and fermentation rolls along.

But the recipe creators didn't know this. Was it an incredible amount of trial-and-error or a few homebound Edisons and Curies?

SWEET YEAST DOUGH

So yeast needs some sugar. But a very high concentration of sugar in sweet doughs slows down, rather than helps, the yeast. The scarce resource is water, and both yeast and sugar compete for it, urged on by a force of nature, osmosis.

Fish cookery, as we have seen, involves life-and-death changes caused by osmosis, and the situation with yeast is comparable. And if osmosis dies, fermentation stops. In a sweet dough, the liquid holds a great deal of dissolved sugar, and the osmotic force tends to push water *out* of the yeast cell, trying futilely to dilute this sugar, but instead overconcentrating the cell's fluids. The flow should be in the other direction, carrying water and dissolved sugar *into* the yeast cell to be changed and expelled as CO_2 and ethyl alcohol. The yeast, its efficiency lowered, its food (sugar) flowing *away* from it, is fighting an uphill battle. All we can do is increase the amount of yeast to get the gas production back up to par.

101. RASPBERRY LOAF

(2 small 9-inch × 5-inch loaves)

- □ 2 packages (8 grams each) dry yeast
- □ 1 cup *warm* water (105–110°F/40–46°C)
- □ 2 teaspoons sugar
- □ 1 cup sugar
- □ 1 cup raspberry jam
- □ 4 tablespoons butter
- 1 teaspoon salt
- □ 4 cups all-purpose flour
- □ 3 eggs

(a) *Activating the yeast:* Put the warm water (warm on the inside of the wrist), the yeast, and 2 teaspoons of sugar in a warm bowl. Stir until well mixed, let stand 10 minutes, then stir up again.

(b) *Dissolving the other ingredients:* In another mixing bowl combine the sugar, ½ cup of raspberry jam, the butter, salt, and the eggs. When well mixed, add the yeast mixture from the first bowl.

Follow directions **(c)** to **(g)** of Recipe 99, White Bread, but set temperature to 350°F.

Make long cuts in the tops of the loaves and spoon the remaining ½ cup of jam into them.

Bake for 50 to 60 minutes at 350°F or until a cake tester comes out dry.

As in many similar recipes—for coffee cakes, for example—there is almost twice as much yeast per cup of flour as in bread recipes. So if you are adapting a recipe, remember to adjust the yeast in accordance with the sugar contents.

SALT-FREE BREAD

Those unfortunates on a salt-free diet are going to have a rough time baking bread.

Sweet doughs and salt-free ones are on opposite ends of the osmotic seesaw. In the salt-free case, the dough liquids have fewer dissolved substances, and the osmotic flow is reversed, driving sugar into the cell, and fermentation is promoted rather than retarded. As with recipes using potato water or too much yeast, salt-free dough may rise too quickly, before the good flavor compounds have been synthesized. So reduce the amount of yeast and be prepared for faster risings.

The real problem with breadmaking is not the work, it's the time it takes. (People who are efficient could bake a few weeks' supply and then freeze. Do *not* store bread in the refrigerator; it stales fastest at temperatures just above the freezing point. Store it in the freezer or at room temperature and heat it just before serving.) A recipe with two risings takes about three hours *before* going into the oven. If that is too long for you to wait, there is still, happily, an escape from the commercial bread rut. It is quick bread. These are breads that use chemical agents for leavening, as do most cakes.

QUICK BREADS

Chemical leavening depends on a basic (alkaline) chemical, sodium bicarbonate (also called baking soda), which when heated decomposes into washing soda, carbon dioxide, and water. This leaven turns out dismal stuff, often with an off-taste and a spotty yellow color. The same alkaline-sensitive pigments that make white vegetables or rice turn yellow in alkaline cooking water are contained in flour and thus affect the color of bread baked with bicarb.

Even as leavening, sodium bicarbonate doesn't cut the mustard. The molecule is just too stable for the job. It does not decompose soon enough in the baking period, but waits around until the temperature rises, by which time the dough is on its way to setting. It needs an acid rather than heat to decompose it. Thus the bicarbonate is mixed with a dry chemical acid and called baking powder. Baking powder needs only to get wet to start a gas-evolving neutralization reaction:

$$\textit{sodium bicarbonate} + \textit{acid salt} + CO_2 + H_2O$$

The baking powder manufacturer has many acids among which to choose, and double-action baking powder has become a favorite. It actually contains *two* acids. One reacts slowly at room temperature and quickly in the oven, while the other takes up the slack at room temperature. It is easy and quick. To see how baking powder really works, try this experiment.

AUTODEMONSTRATION V

1 tablespoon baking powder
1 tablespoon bicarbonate of soda (baking soda)
2 tablespoons vinegar
2 cups water

Put a cup of water into each of two saucepans. Add baking powder to one, and bicarbonate and then the vinegar to the other. Heat both gently.

Watch out for foaming over! Notice how much more even the gas production is from the baking powder. But a lot of cookbooks have recipes whose leavening arise from combinations of all kinds of acids with bicarbonate of soda. In order to be in a position to decode them, or to concoct our own, let's try some recipes that use homemade versions of baking powder.

Let us set ourselves up in the manufacturing-chemistry business by making soda bread with our own home mixture: baking soda plus a dry acid, cream of tartar.

102. SODA BREAD

(1 9-inch [approx.] square loaf)

- 4 – 4½ cups all-purpose flour
- □ 2 teaspoons cream of tartar
- □ 1 teaspoon baking soda (bicarbonate of soda)
- 2 teaspoons salt
- 2 cups milk
- 2 tablespoons butter, melted
- 1 egg, beaten
- 1 tablespoon sugar

Preheat your oven to 350°F.

Sift the flour, cream of tartar, soda, salt, and sugar together into a bowl. Mix in the milk, egg, and butter, and knead the dough until it is soft. (Add more flour if it is sticky.)

Grease a cookie sheet, shape the dough into a 1-inch slab, score it in a grid pattern with a knife, and bake it for 50 to 60 minutes, or until a cake tester comes out dry.

The quantities of baking soda and cream of tartar are balanced so they will fully consume each other. There is an easy way to tell if there is too much baking soda — the spotty yellow off-color.

Here are a series of recipes that use an acid food to decompose the bicarbonate. Sometimes these acids are difficult to identify, because they do not taste sour.

103. MOLASSES BREAD

(1 large 9-inch × 5-inch loaf)

- □ 2 cups all-purpose flour
- □ 2 teaspoons baking soda (bicarbonate of soda)
- 1 teaspoon salt
- ¼ pound butter, melted but not hot
- ⅓ cup brown sugar
- 2 eggs
- □ ½ cup molasses
- □ ½ cup honey
- 2 teaspoons cinnamon
- ½ cup golden seedless raisins
- 2 tablespoons rum
- □ 2 tablespoons lemon juice

Soak the raisins in the rum and lemon juice overnight.

Preheat the oven to 350°F.

Beat the eggs, molasses, and honey into the brown sugar. Sift the flour, baking soda, salt, and cinnamon together and beat in the butter with a whisk. Blend it into the egg mixture. Mix in the raisins along with the rum and lemon juice.

Pour into a 9-inch dark metal baking pan and bake for 45 minutes or until a cake tester comes out dry.

Molasses, though sweet, is acidic and will neutralize the baking soda, releasing carbon dioxide. Honey is also acidic and will act the same way, as will the lemon juice. Buttermilk, which is sour skim milk, is obviously acidic and can act directly on baking soda. I hate the stuff and will not keep it around, but instead of rejecting a recipe that includes it, I'll either just add 1 to 1¼ teaspoons cream of tartar to each cup of sweet milk, or I will use sweet milk and replace each teaspoon of baking *soda* with 4 teaspoons of baking *powder*. The tables below give equivalences for playing around with substitutions. But remember to adjust the *liquid content* if you substitute a thick ingredient for a thin one.

Table VIII

Acid-Base Equivalences

The following ingredients will be neutralized by ½ teaspoon baking soda (bicarbonate of soda):

1 cup sour milk	1 cup yogurt
1 cup buttermilk	½ cup molasses
1 cup apple sauce	1 tablespoon vinegar
1 cup mashed bananas	1 tablespoon lemon juice
1 cup tart jam	

They are equivalent in acidity to 1 teaspoon cream of tartar.

Table IX

Milk and Baking Powder Acid-Base Equivalences

1 cup sour milk or 1 cup buttermilk	= 1 cup sweet milk +	1 – 1¼ teaspoon cream of tartar or 1 tablespoon vinegar or 1 tablespoon lemon juice
1 cup sour milk or 1 cup buttermilk	+ ½ teaspoon baking soda =	1 cup sweet milk + 2 teaspoons baking powder
1 teaspoon cream of tartar	+ ½ teaspoon baking soda =	2 teaspoons baking powder*

*Each 2 teaspoons of baking powder has ½ teaspoon cornstarch filler.

BISCUITS AND MUFFINS

The commonest examples of baking-powder breads are biscuits and muffins. Biscuits are very simple doughs that are kneaded; muffins are sweeter and are not kneaded. Moreover, people like flaky biscuits, so they are mixed like Pie Pastry, Recipe 98, while muffins are more like little cakes.

104. SESAME BISCUITS
(about 12)

- □ 2 cups all-purpose flour
- □ 3 teaspoons baking powder
- 1 teaspoon salt
- □ ¼ cup butter, *chilled*
- □ ¾ cup milk
- 2 tablespoons caraway seeds
- 2 tablespoons toasted sesame seeds

Chill a mixing bowl, 2 knives (or a pastry blender), a fork, and a rolling pin.

Preheat the oven to 425°F.

Sift the flour, baking powder, and salt together into the chilled bowl. *Cut in* the butter *with the chilled knives or pastry blender* until the dough looks mealy. Mix in the milk and seeds with the fork.

Knead the dough *gently and very little, less than a minute,* on a floured surface. Roll it out with the chilled pin and cut out 12 rounds with a cookie cutter. Place them on a greased cookie sheet and bake for 12 to 20 minutes.

If biscuit is enriched with egg, sugar, and more liquid, it can be a muffin batter and will be handled very differently—that is to say, hardly at all.

105. MAPLE MUFFINS
(about 12)

- □ 2 cups all-purpose flour
- □ 3 teaspoons baking powder
- 1 teaspoon salt
- ¼ cup butter or margarine, melted but not hot
- ¾ cup milk
- 1 egg, lightly beaten
- ½ cup maple syrup
- ⅓ cup cream

Preheat the oven to 400°F.

Sift the solids together in a mixing bowl. Add in the liquids with *as little mixing as is necessary to combine everything*. The batter should be lumpy, not smooth.

Spoon it into the cups of a greased muffin tin and bake for 25 minutes.

The crucial element is the flour-liquid ratio. In muffins it is ideal for gluten formation, but not much gluten is needed here. The egg protein builds up all the structural framework that is wanted, so gluten is unnecessary and even unwelcome. Too much "structure" will toughen the dough and also, by trapping gas in the muffin cup, create elongated vertical gas cells, "tunnels." So the idea is to prevent gluten formation by reducing mixing to a bare minimum. Like a self-conscious lover, the muffin mixer struggles toward tenderness by reducing the handling. When I feel I am going to be a heavy-handed mixer, I increase the sugar or fat a bit to retard the gluten development.

CAKES

Muffins may not be examples of refined cuisine, but they are interesting as the "missing link" between bread and cake. The most significant change in the transition from sandwich to shortcake is the *kind* of flour used. Bread flour is 12 – 14 percent protein, cake flour is only 7.5 percent, and all-purpose flour is 10 percent protein. Cake flour is protein-poor and holds down the gluten content because we like cakes that break rather than tear, that are more delicate than durable. And since cake batter is less tenacious and elastic, it cannot trap and hold carbon dioxide gas as easily as bread dough; so most cake recipes use baking powder.

Cakes are easy items to cook at home, usually taking less preparation time than most main dishes. And they are excellent vehicles for the exercise of a baroque imagination. But the passionate baker should keep a few principles in mind when concocting The Miracle.

Cakes can range from very low egg content, with milk to supply liquid, to high egg content with less milk. The next two recipes are from opposite ends of this scale.

106. SPICE CAKE

(2 9-inch × 5-inch loaves)

- □ 1 cup butter or margarine, at room temperature
- □ 2 cups sugar
- □ 4 eggs
- □ 4 cups *cake* flour
- □ 4 teaspoons baking powder
- 1 teaspoon salt
- □ 1⅓ cups milk
- 1 teaspoon ground ginger
- 1 teaspoon ground cinnamon
- ½ teaspoon ground nutmeg
- ¼ teaspoon ground cloves

Preheat the oven to 350°F.

Cream together the butter and sugar, then mix in the eggs one by one. Sift together the flour, baking powder, salt, and spices. Add portions of this alternately with portions of the milk, to the egg mixture. Mix well but *do not overstir.* Pour into two 9-inch × 5-inch dark metal cake pans.

Bake for 45 minutes or until a cake tester comes out dry.

107. APRICOT POUND CAKE

(2 8-inch × 8-inch loaves)

- □ ¾ pound butter or margarine, at room temperature
- □ 3 cups sugar
- □ 8 eggs
- □ 4 cups *cake* flour
- □ 4 teaspoons baking powder
- 1 teaspoon salt
- □ 1 cup milk
- ½ cup apricot jam

Preheat the oven to 350°F.

Cream together the butter and sugar, then beat in the eggs one by one.

Sift together the flour, baking powder, and salt and add portions of this alternately with portions of the milk to the egg mixture.

Pour the batter into two greased 8-inch × 8-inch × 2-inch dark metal cake pans and bake for 50 minutes or until a cake tester comes out dry. Let the cakes cool.

Heat the jam in a saucepan and smear a thin layer on the cakes.

Suppose I have a nice recipe that bakes well, tastes good, and is easy to make, but I want to make it richer with more eggs. I can't just add some more eggs to the batter and hope it will turn out as well. The eggs change the quantity of liquid in the recipe — they are mostly water themselves — so I have to alter the proportions of other ingredients to bring the recipe back into balance. These rearrangements are easier to see if I tabulate the ingredients of these two cake recipes.

Table X
Cake Ingredients

	Spice	*Pound*
cups flour	4	4
eggs	□ 4	□ 8
cups fat	□ 1	□ 1½
cups milk	□ 1⅓	□ 1
cups sugar	2	3
teaspoons baking powder	4	4

Fats and eggs increase together, but as a consequence, the milk content goes down. Egg and milk are balanced to keep the total amount of liquid (and the viscosity) fairly constant. In Recipe 98, Pie Pastry, fat tenderized the dough by interfering with gluten formation, and so broke down the dough's cohesiveness. In the recipe for pound cake, something has to hold things together, and the high fat level ensures that it will not be gluten. So eggs must be included to assume the structure-forming function. The benefits are reciprocal, because the lecithin of the egg helps emulsify the fat into the water-based batter and keeps it from leaking out.

This is obviously a system of checks and balances. If you modify an ingredient, the texture will change, so to reproduce a texture you like, you will most likely have to modify *two* ingredients. To help you do this, refer to Table XI, which lists the texture-changing effects of the most sensitive ingredients.

And remember that you can substitute ⅞ cup of all-purpose flour for each cup of cake flour.

Now you are ready for relaxed experiments with cake recipes. But remember that these ideas can also be a lifesaver on those days when things are looking bleak. If you have planned a cake for dinner and discover, after the stores have closed, that there is no more cake flour in the closet, use all-purpose, or, *in extremis,* even bread flour, and alter the rest of the ingredients toward the "low firmness" category.

Table XI
Cake-Texture Relations

More Firmness	*Less Firmness*
Low fat	High fat
Low liquid	High liquid
High egg content	Low egg content
Acid ingredients (honey, molasses, cream of tartar, buttermilk)	
Low sugar content	High sugar content

Take a low-calorie break every now and then with a cake that contains no butter or shortening and is leavened like a soufflé, by the air beaten into an egg-white foam.

Let's get into this area slowly, with a hybrid cake that is leavened by baking powder *as well as* an egg-white foam.

108. SPONGE CAKE
(one 9-inch or 10-inch tube)

- □ 6 eggs, *separated*
- □ 1 cup sugar
- 2 tablespoons grated orange rind
- 1 tablespoon grated lemon rind
- □ 1 cup *cake* flour
- □ 1 teaspoon baking powder
- ¼ teaspoon salt
- □ ½ teaspoon cream of tartar
- ½ teaspoon vanilla extract
- ½ teaspoon almond extract

Preheat the oven to 350°F.

Beat the egg yolks with ¾ cup of sugar, the orange and lemon rinds, and the two flavorings until thick and lemon colored.

Sift together the flour, baking powder, and salt and mix into the egg mixture.

Beat the egg whites and cream of tartar in a *copper, stainless steel, glass, or ceramic (but not plastic) bowl* until they form soft peaks. Add the remaining ¼ cup of sugar and continue beating until the whites form stiff peaks.

Fold the egg whites *gently* into the batter and blend carefully. Pour *gently* into a 9-inch or 10-inch tube pan.

Bake for 45 minutes or until a cake tester comes out dry.

Invert the cake in the pan until it cools. (Do not let the cake bear any weight; if the pan is too short and the cake protrudes, support the outer rim with some books or slip the tube over a pop bottle.)

This should be very reminiscent of the mousse and soufflé recipes in Chapters 1 and 7. The egg whites are beaten with cream of tartar and sugar to form a stable foam and the other ingredients are folded in to disturb it as little as possible.

Angel Food Cake is almost the same, but is even more ascetic, eliminating all the cholesterol-bearing egg yolks.

Baking, whether a rich cake, a pie, or a soufflé, is a difficult business to time. First, people don't calibrate their ovens. Most I've used have been 50°F off their settings. Buy an oven thermometer, calibrate your oven once a year, and keep the chart by the oven.

Then there are the baking utensils I'm supposed to have. I do not like to spend money on imperishable objects, so I do not own many pots and pans. Consequently, I never seem to own the kind of pan called for by my recipe.

POTS AND PANS
METAL/GLASS/CERAMIC

Pans do more than hold the food together; they are active in the transfer of heat. Usually we can get away with using whatever pots and pans we own if we understand their different interactions with heat.

Heat is transferred in three ways: convection, conduction and radiation. Convection is the process that makes the top tier in a steam bath hotter than the bottom. There is actual movement; hot vapor rises, loses its heat to benches, walls, and paunches, and sinks to the floor. These movements organize themselves into currents of circulating vapor — convection currents. Placing pans in the oven with plenty of space between them will allow these currents to move easily, with good heat transfer.

Conduction is the process of transferring heat from the hot part of an object to its cooler parts, or from a hot one to a cool one in *contact* with it. By this method, heat passes from an oven wall, along a rack, to a pan, through its metal skin, and to the food in contact with the pan's interior.

Spectrum of light radiated by the sun.

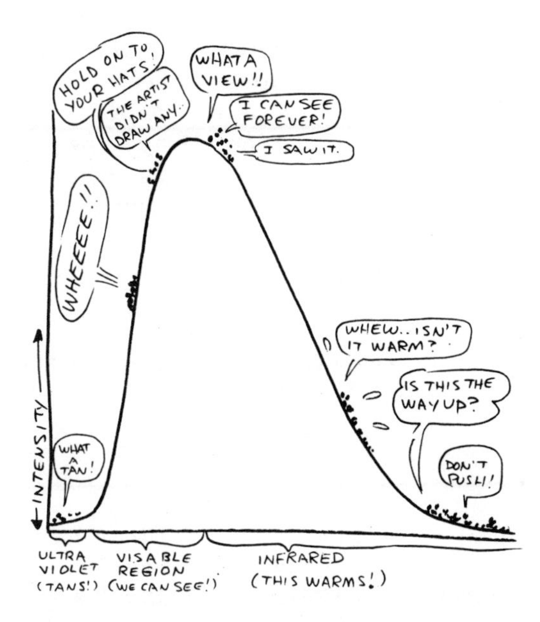

However, the energy transferred in an oven by convection and conduction is relatively minor. Two-thirds to three-quarters of the heat effective in baking gets there by radiation. This is the way the sun's energy reaches the earth; it does not depend on any contact between source and recipient, nor any material movement. Radiant heating uses the energy of light to heat objects. While being drawn up a ski slope on a chairlift, I am warm when in sunlight, but quite chilly as the chair passes into a shaded area, even though the air temperature is the same.

But the different colors that make up sunlight have different effects. The infrared portion of sunlight, out beyond the limit of visibility into the redder-than-red range, is particularly effective in heating and is the major source of radiant heating in an oven. At the other end of the color range, beyond the limit of blue visibility, is the ultraviolet, which causes suntan and sunburn.

Materials differ greatly in their effect on incident light. Infrared and visible light pass through window glass, but ultraviolet light does not. So I can sit by a window in a cool cabin and still be warm, but I will not get tanned. On the other hand, if I want to cool off a cabin heated by sun on summer days, I can put aluminum foil over the windows. It reflects much of the sun's radiation, and the room cools off.

In the same way, a cooking utensil affects the amount of light energy passing through it or absorbed by it, and therefore the speed at which the food bakes. Glass is efficient because infrared radiation passes through it and is absorbed by the food. Polished metal is inefficient because the radiation is reflected away. Metal pans that are dull or dark do not reflect as well as shiny ones and so are more efficient at absorbing radiation. (Dirty snow melts faster than clean snow because it is a better sunlight absorber.)

The following table gives crude adjustments when you are using the "wrong" pan.

Table XII
Oven Temperature Compensations

	Recipe calls for		
You are using	*Bright Metal*	*Dull Metal*	*Glass, Ceramic*
Bright Metal	Same	Use 10° higher	Use 25° higher
Dull Metal	Use 10°F lower	Same	Use 15° higher
Glass, Ceramic	Use 25°F lower	Use 15°F lower	Same

Some materials will suit a recipe better than others. Suppose you are troubled by a custard pie whose bottom crust gets soggy before the custard sets in baking. You could use the principles of custard cookery (p. 133) to make a firmer texture: scalded milk, more egg yolks, less liquid, more acidic ingredients, etc. That's using the food chemistry to give us an advantage. Now we can use physics. By baking with a glass pie plate we get the bottom crust hot and set the custard near it faster than with metal.

But in the case of cookies a dark metal or glass tray may let them brown *too* fast, so bright metal is best in that case.

For a heavier and browner crust use glass, enamel, or dull metal. In fact you can tailor your pan for a particular effect by darkening one part and polishing the rest, or coating part of a glass dish with aluminum foil.

Assured of success by following these scientific guides, your artistic inventiveness can be released in a lush cornucopia of baked delights. Just diet the next day.

CHAPTER 9: RÉSUMÉ

I. UNLEAVENED BREAD

DO:
- Reduce kneading to decrease toughness
- Add butter or shortening to the recipe to decrease toughness

II. PIE PASTRY

DO:
- Make sure these items are *cold*: bowl, utensils, ingredients
- Use utensils that do not conduct much heat (wood or thin metal)
- Use solid fat (butter, lard, solid margarine, shortening)

DON'T:
- Overwork the dough
- Linger over it, letting it warm up
- Use oil or liquid fat

III. LEAVENED DOUGH

DO:
- Use lukewarm water to hydrate and start the yeast
- Grease the bowl
- Remember to punch down the dough
- Add more yeast when sweetening a recipe
- Store bread in the freezer

DON'T:
- Let salt-free bread rise too fast
- Store bread in the refrigerator

IV. QUICK BREAD

DO:

- Remember that baking powder = sodium bicarbonate (baking soda) + acid
- Choose your acids for homemade baking powder from cream of tartar, buttermilk, honey, molasses, vinegar, lemon juice, and other fruit juices
- Knead biscuit dough lightly and quickly
- Add sugar or fat to a recipe to reduce toughness

DON'T:

- Overstir muffin batter

V. CAKES

DO:

- Calibrate your oven with an oven thermometer
- Replace cake flour with all-purpose flour or bread flour (or mixtures thereof) to *increase* cohesiveness
- Change texture by following Table XI on page 167
- Interchange pots and pans by following Table XII on page 170

VI. FOAM-LEAVENED CAKES

Follow the rules for making egg-white foam, namely

DO:

- Use *clean* copper, steel, glass, or ceramic bowls
- Use clean mixing utensils (beaters)
- Use cream of tartar
- Use some sugar (optional protection)

DON'T:

- Use plastic or aluminum bowls
- Use fat-contaminated beaters
- Let *any* egg yolk drop into the whites
- Overbeat whites to the dry stage

10

BEVERAGES: THE DEVIL'S WORKS

I started this book by talking about toast burners and egg misboilers. But I neglected those toilers in the vineyards of instant heartburn, the makers of bad coffee: short-order cooks who seem to recycle their coffee to make it muddier and more bitter; the stuff that leaks out of automatic coin vendors (I suspect it is served in plastic cups because it would corrode metal); those cafeteria push-button numbers that cough out a cup like a hacking chain smoker; and so on.

Actually, there are so many ways to mess up the preparation of coffee that the chances of brewing a good cup seem pretty low. Moreover, tap water too often does not taste good. If one's water is more of a solvent than a refreshment, there is no possibility it will magically become mountain dew when put in a coffee pot. It is even possible to misboil water by overcooking it.

Water has lots of air dissolved in it (about 2 percent of its volume), and the water-air combination has a strange synergistic effect. Liquids taste better when saturated with air, but overboiled water, with all the air driven out of it, has a flat taste and is only good for victims of a wilderness-survival course. In any hot beverage, always use freshly drawn cold water and boil it as little as possible.

109. COFFEE

There are too many ways to make coffee to give one definitive recipe here. But there are several things that should always be seen to:

(a) Keep your coffee maker *scrupulously clean. Rinse it* thoroughly after washing to get rid of the last traces of soap.

(b) Use tap water that has *run for a few seconds. Never use water from the hot water tap or water that has already been boiled.*

(c) *If your tap water does not taste good, use bottled water.* After all, it is your major ingredient.

(d) If possible, *use coffee beans* and grind them *immediately before brewing.*

(e) *Store* coffee (beans or ground) *in the freezer.*

Wash, wash, wash—that's the first rule of good coffeemaking. The utensils should be kept immaculate. Coffee contains oil; it is often visible floating on top of a cup of rich coffee. Oil films are very difficult to remove from metal, and only slightly easier from glass and ceramic. Like any fat this oil can go rancid and generate off-flavors by reacting with oxygen in the air. So washing is critical.

Coffee experts swear by coffee grinders (which also have to be as well scrubbed as the pot), and with good reason. Most of the coffee's flavor constituents are very volatile, and grinding releases them. Ground coffee stored in a paper sack at room temperature will quickly lose its taste. Far better to put into a hermetically sealed Mason jar in the refrigerator or freezer, where the low temperature keeps the volatility down.

Another serious loss of volatile components occurs during roasting. It is necessary to roast the beans to develop their flavor, but every now and then it is refreshing to do a bit of roasting at home, if you can find a store that sells partially roasted beans (the first roasting disposes of a filmy covering on the bean). Heat some in a saucepan, shaking and stirring constantly, so they do not scorch. When they are dark brown, grind and brew immediately. Or try this version of *café au lait.*

110. COFFEE MILK
(2 cups)

¼ cup coffee beans
2 cups milk
2–4 teaspoons sugar

Put the beans in a grinder and grind *very coarsely* or crush them in a mortar.

Put the milk and coffee in a *heavy* saucepan and *heat gently,* with *constant stirring,* until it *just starts* to boil, but do not let it boil.

Strain it through a cheesecloth-lined fine sieve and sweeten to taste with sugar.

TEA

As a drug, tea is almost as good as coffee. It has anywhere from 30 to 110 percent the caffeine content of coffee, depending on the type of leaf and method of brewing. So it is an excellent stimulant. To appreciate its other properties, taste, color, and aroma, you should make it very carefully.

111. TEA

3–6 teaspoons tea
6 cups *fresh cold* water
sugar, lemon, and cream

Warm a *glass or ceramic* teapot by rinsing it with hot water.

Let the *cold* water tap *run a few seconds,* then fill a tea kettle and heat the water. Put the tea in the teapot. (A little teaball will contain the leaves if they annoy you.) Add the water *just* as it starts to boil and *cover* the teapot.

Brew for 3 minutes, then serve the tea with sugar, lemon, and cream on the side.

Metal, not recommended for coffee makers, is out of the question for tea pots. Tea pigments are polyphenols ("polly-feen-awlz") and react with metal, either of the pot or as minerals dissolved in hard water. In either case a surface film and bitter taste result.

Many of these pigments are in constant equilibrium with another form of themselves. These transvestite molecules can be pushed around by acid, H^+; if the acid concentration is increased, the equilibrium is shifted. This is what happens when lemon juice, a source of H^+, is added to tea. The pigment changes from its highly colored state to its paler sister, and the tea lightens in color dramatically.

HX	H^+ +	X^-
weakly colored pigment	*acid*	*highly colored pigment*

The brewing temperature should be just below the boiling point. If the tea boils, too many astringent compounds (tannins) are released. These compounds are very useful; they tan leather and were once the treatment of choice for burns. For drinking, however, they should be avoided.

On the other hand, if the water temperature is too low (more than 25°F below the boiling point), the steeping time becomes too long to extract the flavor compounds before the bitter tannins. Preheating the pot and covering it conserves the heat so that brewing occurs at the proper temperature—just below the boiling point. A tea cozy has a point even if it looks silly.

A curious habit of the British is serving tea with milk. Ungenerous visitors think them perverse, but milk has a place in tea, scientifically speaking. Many professional tea tasters routinely add milk to their tea, maintaining that it makes the tea far less bitter, allowing them to continue the tasting for a long time. When you look into the chemistry of a milk-tea combination, these "gut" behaviors are quickly justified. Milk proteins attack and surround the tannins, rendering them incapable of contributing their astringency to the tea. Amazing!

MILK

When I heat milk, I am always nervous, for it has so many ways of messing up. Some milk proteins are denatured by heat quite easily, and settle to the bottom of the pan, where they go into their scorching act. The only way to prevent this is very slow heating and constant stirring.

And if I avoid this subsurface catastrophe, there is always the possibility of an ugly "skin" forming on top. Evaporation of water increases the concentration of the other type of milk protein, casein ("kay-seen"), ultimately leaving a scummy solid on the surface. Again, constant stirring is the only defense.

One of my childish dislikes was the cooked flavor of heated milk. Here the noncasein proteins, which are easily denatured and settle out, are to blame. They behave just like egg-white proteins. Their pleasant watery wanderings stop when heat forces them to open up and begin molecular interattachments. Some of these processes are carried so far they produce the settling solids, while the intermediates and byproducts produce the cooked flavor. One use of hot milk where this flavor is successfully masked is hot chocolate.

112. HOT CHOCOLATE

8 ounces semisweet chocolate, broken up
6 cups milk
2 tablespoons sugar
2 teaspoons almond extract
□ 2 cups whipped cream
2 teaspoons cocoa powder

Heat the milk in a *heavy* saucepan *with constant stirring, but do not let it boil.* Add the chocolate and stir it until it is dissolved. Add the sugar and almond extract.

Pour into heated mugs, *top with whipped cream,* and dust with cocoa.

The cooking must be slow and with a great deal of stirring, for chocolate is high in starch, which scorches unless the temperature is kept down. The whipped cream is more than purely decorative and tasty. It forms a barrier to evaporation and thus reduces the rate of formation of surface skin. Marshmallow topping must serve the same purpose, since there is no other reason to put such a tasteless gooey thing under our noses.

Hot chocolate seems an innocuous enough drink, but it is actually a cryptostimulant. It can contain a respectable dose of caffeine and large amounts of a very analogous compound, theobromine (theobromine contains no bromine at all and derives its name from the genus of trees to which the cocoa tree belongs, *Theobroma,* "food for the gods"). Patients with illnesses particularly sensitive to caffeine and theobromine may find cocoa struck off the list of permissible comforts.

ALCOHOL

Compared to chocolate, in fact compared to anything, alcohol is a vicious drug. It has one of the lowest effective-dose/lethal-dose ratios of commonly used substances. That is, there is a very small difference in the amount of alcohol that will get you high and the amount that will kill you. The reason more people do not o.d. on alcohol is that the stomach is very alcohol-sensitive, and rejects it, causing social strife and a mess in the living room.

So the word is "moderate." Give that ill-treated bag of acid-churned refuse, your stomach, a break. You will be doing your brain a good deed as well.

With moderation in mind, we can enjoy the vintner's and distiller's products, which are most welcome on cruel winter days. The next two recipes are among the most popular defrosters of chilled guests.

113. MULLED WINE

- □ 1 bottle dry red wine
- 1 cup freshly brewed tea
- ½ orange, sliced
- 1 lemon, sliced
- 6 tablespoons sugar
- 2 teaspoons cinnamon
- 6 maraschino cherries
- □ 3 tablespoons rum

Heat all the ingredients, *except the wine and rum,* in a *covered* pot just to the boiling point. Reduce the heat and simmer for 5 minutes. Add the wine, re-cover, and heat to a *simmer*. Add the rum, *re-cover* and reheat, if necessary, to *just below* the simmering point.

114. BUTTERED RUM

- 6 cups apple cider
- ½ cup brown sugar
- 2 teaspoons cinnamon
- ½ lemon, sliced
- □ 1 cup rum
- 2 tablespoons butter

Preheat 6 mugs

Heat the cider, sugar, cinnamon, and lemon to the boiling point in a *covered* pot. Reduce the heat and simmer for 5 minutes. Distribute the rum into the 6 preheated mugs, add the hot cider, and garnish with the butter.

We must be very caring with spirits, and the first recipe is as gentle with the booze as possible. When the extraction of flavor from the fruit and spices requires heating, it is done before the addition of the wine. Boiling would drive too much alcohol out of the wine. When the rum is added, the simmering point should not even be reached. The second recipe is even more circumspect; it heats nothing but the flavored cider, and counts on it and the heat retained in the mug to raise the temperature high enough.

You can ignite these drinks if you want to be dashing. The rum has a high alcohol content, but even so, it will not ignite at room temperature. It should be warmed up just the slightest bit.

My only excuse for withholding this dessert until this chapter is that it is flamed. The excuse may be weak, but the recipe is not.

115. CREPES MARRONS

(4 servings)

- 1 cup milk
- 1 egg
- 2 tablespoons bland oil
- ½ teaspoon salt
- 1 cup all-purpose flour
- 1 tablespoon sugar

- 1 small can (9 ounces/ 250 grams) chestnut cream
- 1 tablespoon chocolate syrup
- ½ tablespoon grated orange rind
- 1 tablespoon milk
- ½ teaspoon vanilla extract
- □ ¼ cup rum

Preheat the oven to 350°F.

Combine the first six ingredients in an electric blender until the batter is smooth. Heat a skillet (preferably one with a nonstick coating) over moderate heat and pour about 2 – 3 tablespoons of batter into the pan to form a pancake. When the bottom is brown, turn the crepe and brown the other side. When all the crepes are made, prepare the filling.

Mix the chestnut cream with the chocolate, orange rind, milk, and vanilla extract. Spread this mixture onto each of the crepes. Fold each crepe twice to form a triangle and place them on an ovenproof platter. Heat in the oven for 5 – 10 minutes.

Put the rum in a saucepan and warm *very gently* until the liquid is *slightly warm*. Serve the crepes on their platter, ignite the rum *in the saucepan,* and pour it over the crepes.

Nothing is quite so embarrassing as being unable to light up a flamed dessert. The lights are turned down, the dessert is brought in, the guests exclaim in delight, you touch a match to it — and the match goes out. Another match, a guest's cigarette lighter, and still no ignition. Conversation stops.

There are two ways to turn the odds in your favor. In this recipe the crepes are never allowed to cool off before the big moment. And the liquor is *preheated*. Otherwise you have to depend on the crepes being hot enough to get the alcohol to ignition temperature. To be completely secure, the alcohol is flamed before it is poured over the dessert. That way you can always rush back into the kitchen for another portion of booze if the first one refuses to burn. Don't try to get too much insurance; if you heat the liquor too long, all the alcohol will vaporize away, and there will be nothing flammable near your match.

But these experiments with pyrotechnics and hot drinks can be put aside for the summer months, when cool drinks should be our concern.

The Prince of Coolers is the mint julep, but it takes an iron disregard for self-preservation to suggest a recipe. After *Gourmet* magazine published a mint julep article, it was deluged for months by letters from overwrought readers — recipes, corrections, recollections, rebuttals, threats. . . . But I'm going to offer my version anyway.

116. MINT JULEP
(2 drinks)

3 ounces whiskey (bourbon is traditional but not mandatory)
□ 6 teaspoons super-fine sugar
□ 3 tablespoons mint leaves, *chopped*
2 tablespoons (approx.) water
cracked ice

Chill two cooler glasses in the freezer. Chill the whiskey.

Make a mint *syrup* by crushing the mint leaves with the sugar and dissolving it with the water. *The syrup should be thick.* If it becomes thin, crush more mint with sugar and add it. Strain the syrup and discard the crushed leaves.

Fill the glasses with cracked ice, add the syrup and the whiskey. Put them back in the freezer to allow some of the flavors to intermingle, but do not let the ice melt too much. (About 15 minutes will do.)

We all know that mint is refreshing, but what makes this drink more reviving than, say, ice water, is its low temperature. This recipe makes a thick syrup, and, as we know, such concentrated sugar solutions, like ice cream mixtures, will freeze at temperatures well below 32°F. An alcohol-water mixture will also freeze only at a very low temperature, so when a syrup is added to it, the possibility of a truly subzero drink is apparent.

With more traditional drinks, the concentration of the sugar solution is less important than the time at which it is added.

117. OLD-FASHIONED
(2 portions)

□ ½ cup water
□ 4 teaspoons super-fine sugar
Angostura bitters
lemon peel, 2 pieces
1 cup soda water
2 maraschino cherries
⅔ cup whiskey
ice

Dissolve the sugar in the water with a few drops of the bitters. Apportion into 2 glasses. Divide the other ingredients into the two glasses, add ice, and *stir well*.

The sugar is dissolved *before* the alcohol is added. Sugar is more than two hundred times less soluble in alcohol than water, so it must be dissolved in the water-based components of the drink. (If you are making a strong drink, with not much water in it, use super-fine. For a real killer your only solution is to use a simple sugar syrup.)

This drink looks best clear, so it must be stirred and not shaken. Shaking, even when it does not produce a foam, dissolves enough minute air bubbles to give the drink a cloudy appearance.

118. BRANDY SOUR
(2 portions)

1 teaspoon lemon juice
2 teaspoons lime juice
□ 4 teaspoons super-fine sugar
½ cup brandy
□ 3 egg whites
1 cup orange juice, strained
□ ice

Dissolve the sugar in the citrus juices. Pour into a shaker, add the brandy, egg whites, and an *ice cube*. Shake vigorously until the drink is foamed.

Put some cracked ice into serving glasses and strain the sour into them.

The ice cube provides some mechanical agitation to help with the foaming.

When a drink contains soda but is foamed, the soda cannot be added before the foam is formed, for it will lose its effervescence if shaken.

119. SEASIDE FOAMER
(1 drink)

2 ounces vodka, chilled
2 ounces orange juice, chilled
2 teaspoons super-fine sugar
□ 1 egg white
□ ice
soda water

Mix the first three ingredients in a shaker. Add the egg white *and an ice cube* and *shake until the drink foams*. Strain into a tall glass and top off with soda water.

The commonest foamy drink is, of course, beer. As with all foams, cleanliness is of great importance. Any spare detergent or grease on the glass will break the foam very quickly.

A curious story is told about the life-saving effect of beer foam. Among the chemicals that will destroy a foam is acetone (nail polish remover), which is also present in the body chemistry of diabetics and can sometimes be smelled on their breath. But even when present at levels below detection by smell, the acetone will kill a beer foam. So when a drinking doctor noticed that one of his barmates was always drinking headless beer, he urged him to get a checkup for diabetes. Now he's drinking skim milk.

Having used egg whites to make foamy cocktails, it is nice to find a use for the yolks.

120. POST-COITAL RESTORER
(1 drink)

¼ cup Advocaat or other egg-based liqueur
¼ cup cream
1 egg yolk

Add the ingredients, in the order given, to a glass. (Slip the yolk in by tilting the glass.) Drink this concoction without mixing it.

In the same spirit, may I offer a variation on the Mexican ritual with tequila: lick some salt, swallow a shot of tequila, and bite a wedge of lemon. In my refinement, natural organic materials are emphasized.

121. MEXICAN PACIFIER

1 (or more, to taste) beautiful friend
sea
tequila
lemon, cut in wedges

Go into the sea with your friend. Emerge, but do not towel. Lick a portion of your friend, swallow a shot of tequila, and bite a lemon wedge. Repeat until peaceful.

CHAPTER 10: RÉSUMÉ

I. COFFEE

DO:
- Use *cold* tap water
- Use a coffee grinder if possible
- Keep coffee tightly stored
- Clean the coffee grinder and coffee pot scrupulously and often

DON'T:
- Overboil the water
- Use very hard water
- Use a metal coffee pot if a glass or ceramic one is available

II. TEA

DO:
- Use *cold* tap water
- Preheat the teapot
- Brew with *boiling* water
- Use a tea cozy if possible
- Add milk to reduce bitterness

DON'T:
- Overboil the water
- Use very hard water
- Use a metal teapot
- Overbrew

III. CHOCOLATE

DO:
- Cook over a low heat
- Stir to avoid scorching
- Foam it or cover it to prevent surface skin formation

IV. ALCOHOL

A. Hot Drinks

DO:
- Add the alcohol part last
- Preheat the serving glass or mug

DON'T:
- Heat the fully prepared drink

B. Flamed Desserts

DO:
- Preheat the alcohol part
- Add the alcohol part to a *hot* dessert
- Use a warmed platter or serving dish
- Ignite the alcohol part before pouring it on the dessert

C. Cold Drinks

DO:
- Make a thick syrup for juleps and other supercold drinks
- Dissolve sugar in the water-based ingredients before adding the alcohol
- Use super-fine sugar to make the dissolving easier
- Use sugar syrup if the drink does not contain much water or if it is not to be stirred
- Add soda last to conserve effervescence

DON'T:
- Shake a drink that is to be served clear
- Try to foam a drink in a receptacle that might be coated with a bit of grease or oil

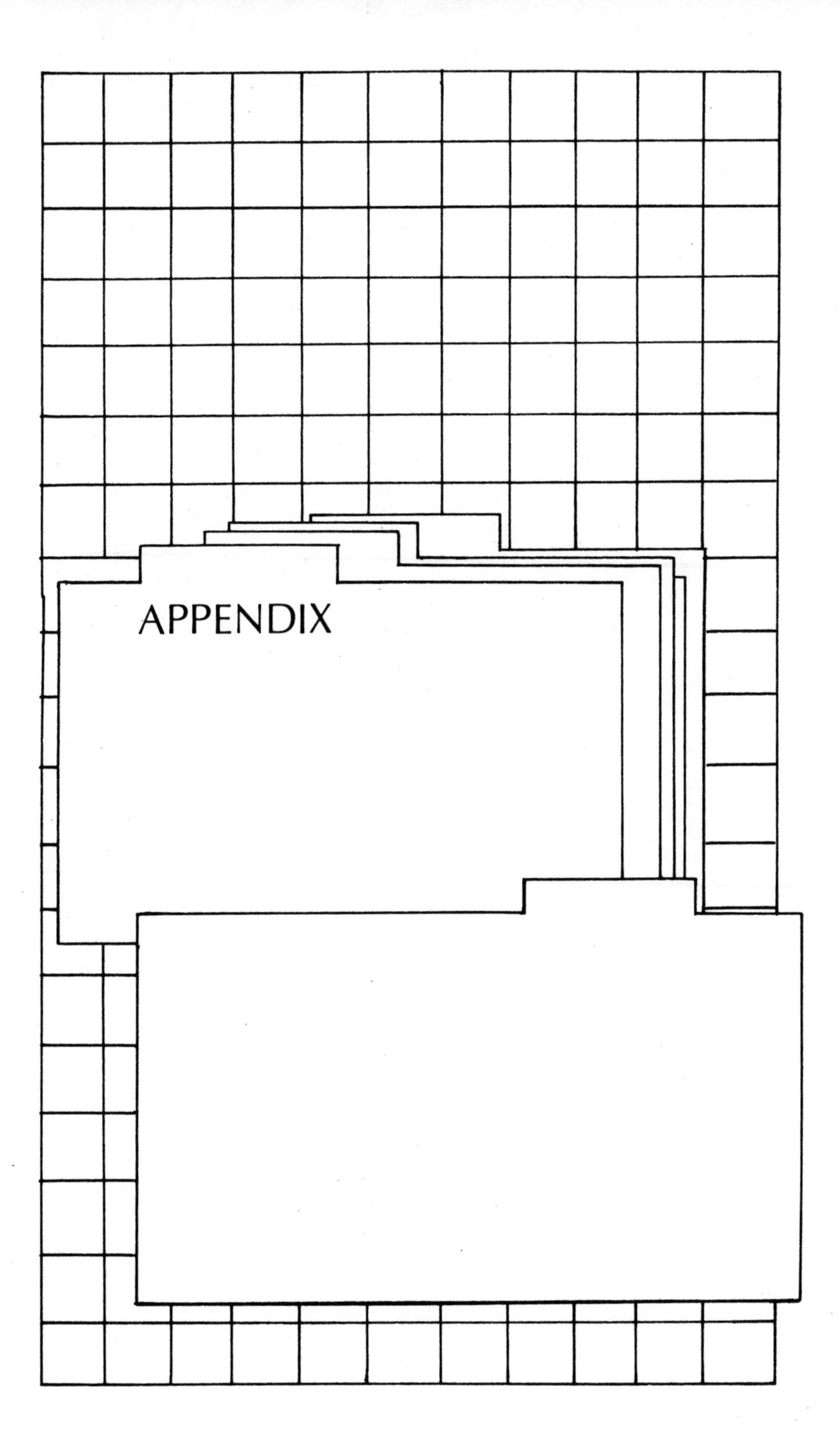
APPENDIX

METRIC AND OTHER EQUIVALENCES IN MEASUREMENT

I. Weight (metric equivalents are approximate)

Ounces (oz.)	=	*Pounds (lb.)*	=	*Grams (g)*	=	*Kilograms (kg)*
1		1/16		28		
2		1/8		57		
3		3/16		85		
4		1/4		110		
5		5/16		140		
6		3/8		170		
7		7/16		200		
8		1/2		230		0.23
9		9/16		255		0.255
10		5/8		280		0.28
12		3/4		340		0.34
14		7/8		400		0.40
16		1		454		0.454
		2		910		0.91
		3				1.4
		4				1.8
		5				2.3

Grams (*g*)	=	*Ounces* (*oz.*)
50		1.8
100		3.5
200		7.1
300		11
400		14
500		18 or 1 lb. 2 oz.

Kilograms (*kg*)	=	*Pounds and Ounces* (*lbs. and oz.*)	
0.5		1 lb.,	2 oz.
0.6		1	5
0.7		1	8
0.8		1	12
0.9		2	0
1.0		2	3
2.0		4	7
3.0		6	10
4.0		8	13
5.0		11	0

II. Volume (U.S. measure and approximate metric equivalents)

Ounces (*oz.*)	*Teaspoons* (*t*)	*Tablespoons* (*T*)	*Cups*	*Milliliters* (*ml*)	*Deciliters* (*dl*)	*Liters* (*l*)
	⅛			⅝		
	¼			1¼		
	½			2½		
	1			5		
½	3	1	1/16	15		
1	6	2	⅛	30		
2		4	¼	60		
3		6	⅜	90		
4		8	½	120		
5		10	⅝	150	1.5	0.15
6		12	¾	180	1.8	0.18
7		14	⅞	210	2.1	0.21
8		16	1	240	2.4	0.24
16			2	470	4.7	0.47
24			3	710	7.1	0.71
32			4	946	9.46	0.946

2 cups = 1 pint
4 cups = 1 quart = 32 fluid ounces
4 quarts = 1 gallon
⅓ cup = 5T + 1t

Milliliters (*ml*)	*Deciliters* (*dl*)	*Liters* (*l*)	*Ounces* (*oz.*)	*Cups*
10	0.1	0.01	0.34	
100	1.0	0.1	3.4	0.42
500	5	0.5	17	2.1
1000	10	1.0	34	4.2

U.S. — English Equivalents

U.S.		=	*English*
1¼	teaspoon	1	teaspoon
1¼	tablespoon	1	tablespoon
1	fl. oz.	1.04	Imperial fl. oz.
0.96	fl. oz.	1.00	Imperial fl. oz.
8	ounce = 1 cup	5/6	breakfast cup
9.6	oz.	1	breakfast cup = 284 ml = 10 Imperial fluid ounces

III. Temperature

	Fahrenheit (°F)	=	*Celsius or Centigrade* (°C)
Pure water freezes	32		0
Pure water boils at sea level	212		100
Syrup tests:			
jelly	220		104
soft-ball	234		112
firm-ball	245		118
hard-ball	250		121
soft-crack	265		129
hard-crack	290		143
Oven temperature:			
	300		149
	325		163
	350		177
	375		191
	400		204
	425		218
	450		232
	500		260
	550		288

III. Temperature (cont.)

Fahrenheit (*°F*)	=	*Celsius or Centigrade* (*°C*)
257		125
302		150
320		160
338		170
356		180
374		190
392		200
428		220
464		240
482		250

IV. Length (for pan sizes): Approximate Equivalents

Inch (″)	=	*Centimeter* (cm)
1		2.5
2		5.1
3		7.6
4		10
5		13
6		15
7		18
8		20
9		23
10		25
11		28
12		30

Centimeter (cm)	=	*Inch* (")
1		0.4
2		0.8
3		1.2
4		1.6
5		2.0
6		2.4
7		2.8
8		3.2
9		3.5
10		4.0
20		7.9
30		12
40		16
50		20

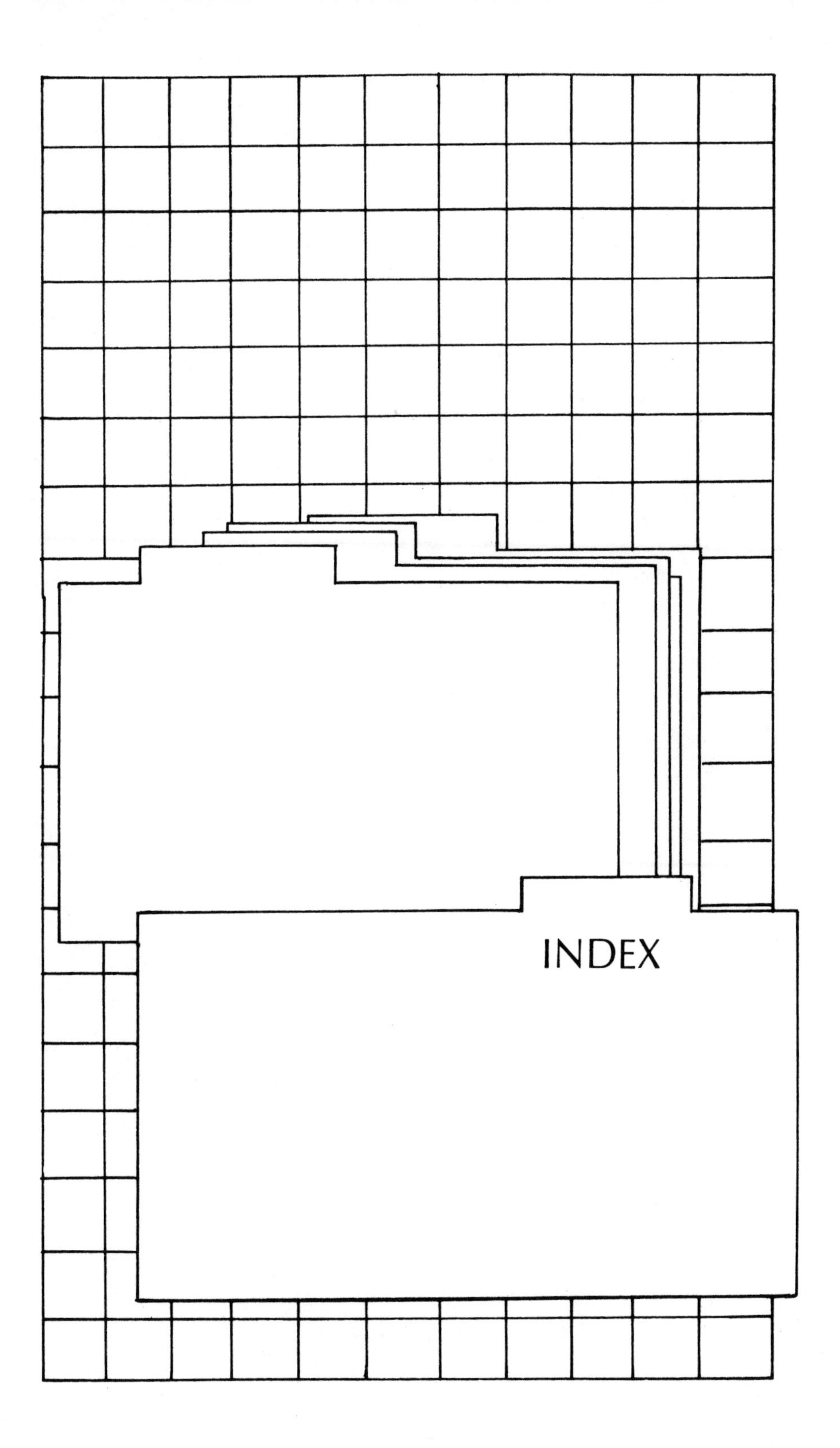
INDEX

Recipe numbers are given in parentheses